# POLICING
# HAMPSHIRE
## and the
# ISLE OF WIGHT

## A Photographic History

One of the original police stations in Portsmouth. Situated in St George's Square, Portsea, it was built in 1843 at a cost of £310 8s. 10d. When the police vacated the building, it was used by the PDSA. It was finally demolished in the 1960s.

# POLICING
# HAMPSHIRE
and the
# ISLE OF WIGHT

## A Photographic History

John Lee, Colin Peake,
Derek Stevens and Clifford Williams

# PHILLIMORE

2001

Published by
PHILLIMORE & CO. LTD.
Shopwyke Manor Barn, Chichester, West Sussex

ISBN 1 86077 196 3

Printed and bound in Great Britain by
BUTLER AND TANNER LTD.
London and Frome

# CONTENTS

## INTRODUCTION

## THE PLATES

*This book is dedicated to all serving, retired and past members of the Hampshire Constabulary and its constituent forces.*

# ACKNOWLEDGEMENTS

Members of the Hampshire Constabulary History Society, past and present, have over the years helped to sort photographs and identify individuals and locations. However, in the last couple of years, the four named authors have spent some considerable time researching the subject matter of the photographs and writing suitable captions for them. Kelvin Shipp has also been particularly helpful in the identification of dates, made possible by his detailed knowledge of uniforms and medals. Alan Barnard, Dave Daisy, Ray Tilling, Bob Cameron, Arthur Bever, Terry Swetnam and Steve Woodward have also given up their free time to help with the process.

The majority of the photographs belong to Hampshire Constabulary. They were either taken by our photographers or were inherited from the Borough and City Forces that have amalgamated with us over the years. We are very grateful to the police photographers from the various forces, who are too numerous to name. However, Nick Scott, recently retired from the Hampshire Force, was of great assistance in identifying various stockpiles of photographs around the Force, which are now safely stored at the Hampshire Record Office (HRO). The HRO have assisted not only with the safe storage of the photographic collection, but also by offering facilities for the society members to meet and conduct their research. The constabulary photographs held by HRO are not currently accessible to members of the public. However Hampshire Constabulary History Society (as a member of the Hampshire Archives Trust) is participating in the Hampshire Photographic Project which will result in a large collection of photographs, including some from this book, becoming accessible through the HRO website.

We would like to thank the following people for loaning or donating photographs: Mrs Lyall (photo 42); Roy Clarke (photos 27 and 72); Phil Burner (photo 21); Ian Beatty (cover and photo 23); Laurie Peake (photo 104); Southern News Service (photo 144).

Many other photographs have been donated to the Force by officers or their relatives. We are very grateful that they donated memories of their police service to the Force History Society.

We would also like to thank the Chief Constable of Hampshire Constabulary for his continued support for the History Society, providing an annual grant to enable us to function and to complete projects, such as the publication of this book.

Finally, the authors would like to point out that every effort has been taken to identify correctly the individual officers in the photographs. However, it is likely that there will be people who have been incorrectly identified, or not identified. We apologise for that. We would ask that, if readers have any further details of any person or location in the book, they send them to the Force History Society. Every attempt has been made to identify and acknowledge sources of photographs used in this publication.

# LIST OF SUBSCRIBERS

Tina Angus
PC 2028 Roger Aplin
PC Alec Ashbolt
Sergeant 5537 Ian Ashbolt
DC Bob Ashton
Maurice Baily, Portsmouth and Hampshire
Chief Inspector Jill Baldry
Superintendent Peter Baldry
Jeff Ballard
David G. Basson, QPM, LL.B
Owen A. Bates, QPM
Peter Beasley
John S. Beel
Nicola Bell (WPC 796)
Mr Jim Bettley
Allan Bissell, retired Sergeant
PC Bob Blake
Syd Blake
Jeff Booth, ex PC 360
John Bradley, fleet manager
Jan Brayley, photographer
Ian Brett
Stephen Arthur James Brewer
Rod Briggs, PC 1171 (Hampshire)
Wayne Brook
Inspector Keith Brown
Norman F. Brown
Barry Sidney Brunsden
Pete Brunskill, Southampton Central
Kevin Budd
Marian Bunker
David Burgess
Philip Dudley Arthur Burner
Len Butcher
Dave Butler, PC 1432 Hampshire (retired)
Bob Cameron
Paddy Carpenter, Chairman – Police Vehicle Enthusiasts' Club
John Carruthers, 1952-82
Nick Carter
PC 2857 Chris Challis, Hampshire Constabulary
Dr Alan Champion
Chief Constable's Office, Hampshire Constabulary
Keith William Cockburn
Supt Paul Colley
William Arthur Coupe
Michael Court
Bill Cox

Mrs. Nanette G.D. Crickmore
PC 423 Tony Croûtear
Valerie Crye
PC Geoff Culbertson, Wildlife Crime Officer
Cllr R. Culver, Hampshire Police Authority
Mrs J.V. Cummings
Norman G. Cunnington
Mark Custerson
Dave and Jackie
Brian Davies, OBE, Asst Ch. Con. 1983-91
PS Tony Davis 1971-2001
Eddie Day
Charlie Dickens
Stephen Andrew Dicker
Brian Dixon
Debbie Donald
Paul Donnellan
Martin F. Dowse (Superintendent retired)
Darren J. Doyle
Jean and Charlie Drane
PC Dave Easson, Southampton and Hampshire
Nigel Eaton, PC 1011
Sandi Ellis
Alan J. Emmott
Vic Ettie
Michael Falls
Lynne Fanton
Guy D. Farmer (serving)
Ian G. Farmer (retired)
Sgt Colin Feeley
DC 105 Terry M. Fitzjohn
Fleet & Farnborough Group of The Hampshire Genealogy Society
WPC Caz Flood
Mark Fogwill
Richard Ford
Stephen Frampton
George W. Franklin
Gerald C. French, ex Chief Superintendent
Gerry French
Julie Furniss BA(Hons)
G. de la Garde
Robert J. Garlike
Keneth Gillett
Richard Glover
Robin Glover
Inspector (retired) Ron Godden

Superintendent Ron Godden
Andrew Golding
James Goodacre
Peter and Debbie Goodall
DC 1374 J.E. Grady (retired)
Clifford Gray
Colin R. Gray
Kenneth M. (Dodger) Green, Superintendent 1975-8
PC 83 Michael John Green
Gerald Gregory
Andrew Grieve
Wᵐ Alan Griffiths
A.C. Grimwood
PC 148 Brian Guest
N. Gwynn, 1948-retired 1977
Brian R. Hailstone
PC 2109 Bryan Haines
Michael E.R. Hampton B.E.M.
David Hanna
June Mary Harris
John Graham Harrison (PC 1694 retired)
Alison Hart
John Harvey, QGM
Charlie Hayward (ex PC 2368)
Geoff Hewett
DC 1007 Tony Hewitt
Michael James Hinchey
Roger Hoddinott
Patrick Holdaway
David Holt
Peter William Holt
Brian D. Homans
Chief Inspector Philip Horn (retired)
Nigel J. Horton, PC 273
P.A. Hughes
Andy Humphreys
Chief Superintendent John A. Hyde
Eric Illingworth
Inspector Richard Ironmonger
Sergeant Alan Jackson
PC Dick Jenkins
PC 2256 Tim Jermyn, Fareham
Albert D. Jewitt
PC 1108 Antony Johnson
PC 588 Bob Johnson (retired)
Brian D. Johnson
Paul Johnson
Ex PC 1371 Chris Jones
Del Jones
DS Phil Jones, Shirley

Teresa Jones, Criminal Justice Manager, Basingstoke
PC 915 Kevin Joyner
Jim Jupe
Sergeant 5924 Parminder Kalirai
Bob Kendall
Paul V. Kilgallon
PC 845 Stefan J. King
Jules Kingshott
Sgt David Knowles
Martin Laux
Supt W.F.J. Lawton, Rtd
John R. Lee
Richard Leedham (DC 2209 SOC 25)
Peter G. Lewis
John P.W. Littlefield
Malcolm Lloyd and Pat Lloyd (Miell)
Charlie Lovegrove, PC 320
Christopher Lovell
Mrs Lynda McCallum Lyall
Superintendent David Lydford
Graham Marshallsay
David R. Martin
Mr Kenneth Martin
David Matthews
Rodney I.J. McCarthy
Ian and Susan McIlwraith
Gavin McMillan (Sergeant-1987)
Peter Metcalf
Guy Milton
Dennis Moore, PC 666 (1964-92)
Inspector Keith Morant, Southampton Bridewell
Graham S. Morey
Gareth Morgan
PC 1401 Jim Mowat
Mrs. Stella Muddiman
National Police Library
PC 2239 Andrew Neilson
Ian P. Newell
PC Andy Noble
Howard Norman
North Hampshire Branch, NARPO
Brian A. Oakshott
Audrey O'Hara
Bryan Oliver
Jim O'Reilly
David A. Owen, PC 1766
Richard J. Owen, Portsmouth F.C. historian
Ex PC 650 Bill Page
Andrew Palacio
David Pallett (retired Chief Superintendent)

Bill Parry (Supt Retd)
Len Payne, retd Chief Superintendent
Colin Peake
Len Pearce
PC 1213 Richard Pennell
Mrs June Perriment
Mr Kevin Perriment
Stephen James Perry
Inspector 5763 Roger Petherbridge
David Pilbeam
Neil Piper
Ray Piper, Portsmouth City Police 1959-67, Hampshire Constabulary 1967-94
Doug Quade
John Rae
Peter Rann
Ian Readhead
James W.M. Reed
Roger H. Reynolds
Chris Richards, PC 774
Steve Ridd, PC 1640
PC 1047 G. Rippon
Inspector 5520 Chris Robinson
Jennifer Kay Robinson
Stephen P. Roman
Bob Rose, C/Insp Hampshire Constabulary 1978
David Rouse (Det. Sgt)
L.E. Ruffell
Captain Robert J. Ruprecht
Doug. Salisbury
Barrie Saunders
PS 5595 Frank Sawle
Roger John Sherborn-Hall
Kelvin Shipp
Sandy Shipway of PPD, CSU, AJD and now CJU, Basingstoke
Irion Noel Sillence
Robert Simpson, ex Portsmouth City Police
Mr and Mrs Skittlethorpe
Jim Small, ex-Sergeant (Havant)
Colin F.W. Smith
David Smith
John W. Smith
D.M. Southwell
Mr and Mrs D. Stevens
Retired PC 622 D.G.P. Stevens
Derek and Jackie Stevens
WPC 2206 Kath Stevens
PC Simon Stocker
Peter Stoddard
G.F. Stratton (PC 841 retired)
Theresa Sumner

Graham Swain, Southampton City and Hampshire, 1947-77 (ex Detective Superintendent)
Terry Swetnam
Geoff Taylor
Jack Taylor
Ralph Taylor, ex Bradford City
Barry Thomas, BT 1600
PC 946 Mark Tidmarsh
Bob Tilley, PC 1672 (retired)
Penelope Tilley
Ray Tilling
Jim Trueman
Miss Mary N.B. Tyrrell
PC Paul Michael Underwood
WPC 361 Julia Veal
Keith Vincent
Robert Royston Waller
Robert G. Ward
Mr. Dave Warner
Ken Warry
David Stanley Warwick
Inspector Antonia Weeks
PC 2492 Weeks 'Shed'
PC 2097 Taff Weller
R.E. Wellington, DC 1839
R.O. West, QPM ACC (retired)
S.E. Weston, PC 199A, Portsmouth City Police
Mr Rodney Whale
Alan Wheeler, QPM 1961-91
Chris White
Mr Darryl F. White
Chief Superintendent Adrian Whiting
Pat and David Willcox
Bill Williams, PC 1610 Hampshire (retired)
Clifford Williams
Harold J. Williams
Robert Williams
Howard Willis
Basil R. Willshire
Mark Wilson
Dick Winter
John A. Winter
Mark Wise
Nigel D. Woodford, PC 2106
Eric B. Woodsford, Chief Insp. (Rtd)
G. Wright
J.A. Wright, QPM, Assistant Chief Constable 1985-95
Simon Wright
Peter and Graham Wyeth

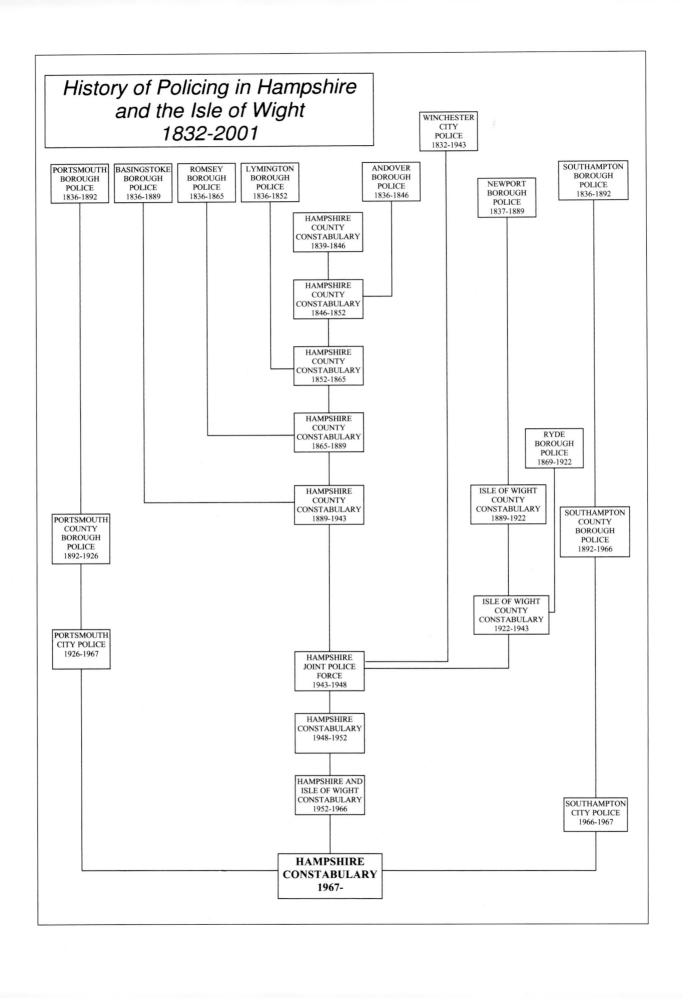

# History of Policing in Hampshire and the Isle of Wight 1832-2001

# INTRODUCTION

## POLICING HAMPSHIRE AND THE ISLE OF WIGHT 1832 TO 2000

The many photographs contained in this book seek to capture the history of the various police forces that make up the current Hampshire Constabulary, a force that covers the two counties of Hampshire and the Isle of Wight. Over the last hundred years or so the smaller Borough and City forces have been absorbed to become part of the larger County Force.

In 1967 the last of many amalgamations took place when Southampton City Police and Portsmouth City Police finally joined the Hampshire and Isle of Wight Constabulary to form Hampshire Constabulary.

## WINCHESTER CITY POLICE

The very first Police Force in Hampshire was the Winchester City Force, formed on 28 July 1832. It consisted of eight officers. Robert Buchanan, the Head Constable, was joined by James Finch, Thomas Ellery, William Shedman, William Masters, William Scorey, Thomas Leach and John Browning. Winchester suffered from the same rapid turnover that Hampshire was to experience later, and that was due to drunkenness in the ranks. Only three of the original constables lasted more than the first year. Buchanan, who also left in 1833, was replaced by an ex-Metropolitan officer, William Shepherd. Buchanan had held the rank of Inspector, whilst Shepherd took over as a Superintendent.

Superintendent Shepherd remained in office until 1851 when, on his resignation, he was replaced by Henry Hubbersley, also previously with the Metropolitan Police.

By 1836 several other Borough forces were formed, namely Portsmouth, Basingstoke, Romsey, Lymington, Andover and Southampton. The following year the first police force on the Isle of Wight appeared with the formation of Newport Borough Police.

Winchester City Police remained as a separate entity until 1943 when it joined the county force. This book contains photographs of Winchester City officers, including the last but one Head Constable, William Stratton.

## HAMPSHIRE CONSTABULARY

Hampshire Constabulary was formed as a result of the County Police Act 1839. In 1836 a Royal Commission of three persons, which included Edwin Chadwick, considered the best means of establishing a rural constabulary. As a result Justices of the Peace were enabled by the Act to maintain a paid police force for the County. At a meeting at Winchester it was resolved that Hampshire should adopt the provisions of the Act and form its own Constabulary. It was to consist of a Chief Constable, 14 Superintendents and 91 constables.

The Chief Constable was to receive £300 per annum, but was also allowed £100 for the purchase and forage for two horses. Two superintendents, one for Headquarters in Winchester and one for the Isle of Wight, were to receive £120 per annum. The remaining Superintendents got the princely sum of £75 per year. In the early days there were three classes of constable, first, second and third. They received 21, 19 and 18 shillings a week respectively. Each Superintendent was allowed access to a horse whilst the constables were provided with uniforms.

Captain George Robbins from Hythe in Hampshire was appointed Chief Constable and the first police constables were Samuel Whitehouse, a soldier from Whitechapel in

London; Robert Messenger, a shoemaker from Bath; John Wigmore, a labourer from Croydon, and a PC John Callingham from the Metropolitan Police.

Discipline was harsh in the early days and did not really start to relax until the 1970s. Whilst promotion could be swift, so could demotion and in many cases dismissal. Without any form of communication, officers were left very much to their own devices. However, there was a strict requirement for them to 'make points' which was where they would meet their sergeant at a set time and at a given location. Failure to make these points often resulted in fines or, if the failure was persistent, dismissal. When the officers did meet their sergeants, many were drunk or were found in circumstances that were not appropriate. Many officers were disciplined for drunkenness or for allowing themselves to be treated (i.e. receiving gifts of any kind).

Restrictions on officers' private lives were equally strict and, again, these remained in force for many decades. It was a requirement up until the late 1980s for officers to ask permission as to where they could live or whether they could get married. The behaviour of wives was often commented upon and held against the officer in question.

A selection of entries from officers' personal records reflects the variety of misdemeanours and associated punishments which ranged from cautions and small fines to dismissal and sentences to Hard Labour.

Charles Walter STEVENS 324
26th July 1904
Having allowed himself to be treated with whiskey when on duty at Holybourne Club Fete on the 20th July 1904.
Fined one week's pay.

Josiah Arthur BETTERIDGE 329
22nd Jan 1908
Committing a breach of Article 17 sec I Instruction Book by getting married without first obtaining the permission of the Chief Constable.
Fined one week's pay and placed at the bottom of the list of constables awaiting married stations.

Charles SMITH 334
3rd Feb 1902
(1)  Being engaged in idle conversation with a prostitute against whom there are 25 convictions whilst on duty on the 21st ulto.
(2)  Telling a falsehood to Inspector White when asked for an explanation of his conduct.
Fined one week's pay.

Archibald Thomas BACON 108
9th Jan 1902
Drunk on duty at Alton on the 25th ulto and publicly disgracing himself by attempting to arrest a sober man on a charge of drunkenness.
Dismissed.

Horace Jesse LONG 348
12th Sep 1903
Having at 12.45 am on the 12th inst been found in a doorway at the Quadrant, Bournemouth in a helpless drunken condition when he should have been at his station on the completion of his duty.
Dismissed.

Albert Harry PEARCE 277
25th Jan 1905
Riding his bicycle on the footpath and allowing himself to be treated to a glass of beer.
Permitted to resign.

William George MILLS 21
1st Dec 1905
Having between the 23rd and 30th Sept 1905 been guilty of conduct likely to bring discredit upon the force by taking an old cloth from a clothes line to wipe his boots with and then throwing it away.
Fined one week's pay.

Charles KNIGHT 158
8th Mar 1872
Associating and drinking with a member of a family of thieves on the 4th inst, for having been drunk and conveyed in a helpless state to the police station at Totton.
Fined a weeks pay and returned to the second class.

Thomas OLDFIELD 213
5th Dec 1862
Absenting himself from his station without leave and telling a gross falsehood, viz: that his wife was dying. Whereas she was in perfect health and going to her work at a stay factory.
Fined a week's pay and dismissed.

Thomas THORNELL 183
8th Aug 1860
Trimming the horse's legs with scissors.
Fined £1.

George WEARN 62
29th Mar 1869
Misconducting himself when on leave of absence on the night of the 27th inst and it having come to the knowledge of the Chief Constable that neither he nor his relatives are respectable.
Dismissed.

Charles TUBB 223
1st Nov 1871
Called on to resign in consequence of the improper connections of his wife.

Daniel FARMER 81
10th May 1840
Dismissed for not assisting PC Wm Sanders 55 in the execution of his duty having run away from him when he was assaulted by a mob on the night of the 9th May inst at the Cart and Horses Kings Worthy.
Pay forfeited.

George CARTER 228
28th Oct 1899
For having been found at 3.40am on the 12 inst. asleep in a cab in the yard of the Pembroke Hotel, Bournemouth when he should have been on duty in Commercial Road.
Reduced to the 3rd Class and cautioned.

Frank BOULTON 165
9th May 1898
Being at the back gate at Gosport Police Station at 12.50am in company with a married woman when he should have been in bed having come off duty at 12pm.
Fined 3 days' pay and cautioned.

Meredith PUGH 210
2nd Sep 1906
Drinking in a public house at Sherfield on the 25 Aug '06 whilst on duty with a man whom he at the time suspected and afterwards arrested for larceny.
Reduced to the 2nd Class.

John PULLEN 4
3rd May 1909
(1) Having consumed liquor in two public houses on his beat when making enquiries whilst performing plain clothes duty on the 26th ultimo.
(2) Accepting liquor from two other persons on the same date when on duty making enquiries which caused him to fall from his bicycle and dislocate his shoulder.
Reduced to the 3rd Class and placed under sick stoppages until fit for duty.

Walter HUNTER 27
14th Jul 1846
Dismissed for being drunk on duty, pay forfeited and sentenced to 7 days' imprisonment with hard labour having failed to deliver over his clothing and appointments at the time and place appointed.

Robert Simpson EDE 85
22nd Jun 1868
Having proved himself incapable of upholding his position as a sergeant and either incapable or unwilling to maintain proper discipline among the constabulary in the district under his immediate charge has been reduced to the rank and pay of a 1st Class PC.

Edward EDNEY 4
18th Jul 1854
Dismissed the Force for getting drunk and in that state allowing a prisoner to effect his escape. Likewise taken before the Magistrates for a violation of duty and sentenced to 14 days' imprisonment with hard labour.

William MOFFAT 144
16th Feb 1914
For having on the 16th inst gravely neglected his duty in not examining a luncheon tray and removing therefrom a knife before allowing a prisoner to have the food whereby he used the knife to cut his throat.
Reduced to the 3rd Class.

Frederick HAWKES Sgt 149
12th Jun 1897
For having showed great want of energy in relinquishing the pursuit of a man wanted for an offence committed in his own division and allowing him to be arrested by a member of the Dorset Constabulary in Hampshire.
Fined one week's pay and cautioned to show more zeal and energy in the future.

William Henry SALE 229
6th Nov 1895
Missing a conference point and being found asleep in the porters room, Railway Station, Cosham on the 30th ultimo when he should have been on duty.
Reduced to the 2nd Class.

George FULLER 140
23rd Feb 1891
Called on to resign as useless.


One means of punishing officers, which is never acknowledged as a formal measure, is the transfer from one posting to another. When officers join the Constabulary they agree to serve anywhere within the force area. Nowadays that is not so much of an issue with excellent motor transport and motorways. However, consider the poor officers from the end of the 19th century who one day were policing Bournemouth and the next were moved to Aldershot. The relative distances, bearing in mind the state of the roads and the lack of motor transport, were enormous. Alternatively, some officers choose to move stations to progress their careers; for example, PC James Hibberd, featured in this book, moved no less than 14 times, from the extreme south west at Lymington to the farthest north east at Aldershot. He served at South Warnborough, Odiham, Lymington, Lyndhurst, Hollybourne, Bournemouth, Cosham, Michelmersh, Hardway, Botley, Basingstoke, Alton, Aldershot and Farley Mount. In those early days the move meant a move of house or lodgings as well as the stress that often causes. Nowadays, with such good transport, officers move station but remain in the same house and travel long distances daily, if required.

By contrast with amalgamations, Hampshire has also lost sections of the force. In 1948 a separate Bournemouth Police Force was created and the local Superintendent, Sydney Bennett, became its first Chief Constable.

## CHIEF CONSTABLES OF HAMPSHIRE

In the 162 years that Hampshire Constabulary has been in existence there have only been 11 Chief Constables. Many of them feature in the main body of this book. Below is a brief pen picture of each Chief Constable, showing where they have worked and served before joining Hampshire.

Captain George ROBBINS (1839-1842) was a Hampshire man, originally from Hythe in the New Forest. Captain Robbins had been a Regular Army Officer and had a very good military career behind him when he took on the role of Chief Constable. He was responsible for turning a group of individuals from a wide range of backgrounds into a disciplined and organised police force. In the early days, as stated previously, the force had to contend with drunkenness among some of its officers and Captain Robbins went to great lengths to deal with the problem by threatening officers found drunk with dismissal or forfeiture of pay. He resigned in 1842.

Captain William Charles HARRIS (1842-1856) was previously a member of the 68th Regiment of Light Infantry and during that time spent four years commanding a detachment employed to aid the civil police in Ireland. He is remembered for the evidence he gave, in 1853, before the Home Affairs Select Committee on Police. The result of this Commission was an act that allowed the amalgamation of police forces, but only if there was mutual consent. In 1856 he resigned to take up appointment as an Assistant Commissioner of the Metropolitan Police. He was remembered and thanked by the Quarter Sessions for improving the organisation of the force, reducing crime and building on the foundations laid by his predecessor. He was also responsible for introducing beat working in 1844.

Captain John Henry FORREST (1856-1891) was previously in charge of the Nottingham Police. He brought with him a reputation of being something of a martinet and a strict disciplinarian. By 1855 the force strength had increased from its original 106 to 235 officers. He retired in March 1891.

Captain Peregrine Henry Thomas FELLOWES (1891-1893) was 40 years old when he took over. He had served at the Military College at Sandhurst and was a member of the 31st (East Surrey) Regiment in 1873. He was made Adjutant in 1880. He served in Australia where he was made Deputy Assistant Adjutant General with a local rank of First Major. He then became Assistant Adjutant General with a local rank of Lieutenant Colonel. He was also for some time stationed at Tipperary in Ireland.

At the beginning of October 1893 he was seriously injured in Winchester when he bravely attempted to stop a runaway horse. The horse and trap were careering down the steep hill past police headquarters. Captain Fellowes, who was off duty, joined three constables and together they tried to form a line across the road to stop the horse. Unfortunately Captain Fellowes was crushed against the stone wall of HQ by the trap and, after a few weeks, he died of severe internal injuries.

Major St Andrew Bruce WARDE (1894-1928) was appointed on 26 February 1894. He saw the force through the turn of the century, through the Great War and was in office as the onset of motorised transport began to have an influence on policing. He retired from ill health in December 1928 and died on 1 December 1929.

Major Ernest Radcliffe COCKBURN (1928-1942) was educated in Harrow and joined the Regular Army in 1894. In 1898 he was a Lieutenant in the 2nd Wiltshire Regiment and served in the South Africa War during which time he was awarded special promotion for distinguished service in the field. He also served in the Manchester Regiment. When he left the army in 1919 he was appointed the Chief Constable of Ayr, before moving to Hampshire in 1928, having been selected from 130 applicants. In 1938 he was awarded the CBE and he retired in May 1942.

Richard Dawney LEMON (1942-1962) was appointed as Chief Constable in June 1942. He was educated at Uppingham and Sandhurst. He was in the West Yorkshire Regiment for three years. In 1934 he joined the Metropolitan Police. He stayed with the Met until 1937 when he moved to Leicester as an Inspector. In 1939 he was appointed ACC in East Riding. He is remembered for creating the Criminal Investigation Department (CID). He left Hampshire to become the Chief Constable of Kent Police.

Douglas OSMOND (1962-1977) was Chief Constable of Shropshire from 1946. During the war he was in the police in London. He served in the Royal Navy during the war and was later a member of the Control Commission in Germany. Douglas Osmond was Chief Constable at the time of the final amalgamations when the two cities of Portsmouth and Southampton joined Hampshire. He was knighted in 1976 and retired in 1977.

John DUKE (1977-1988) came to Hampshire in 1977 from Essex Police. He was responsible for introducing Air Support into the force with the acquisition of the fixed wing aircraft Optica. He retired in 1988 and died in 1989 leaving a widow Glenys and four daughters.

John HODDINOTT (1988-1999) Both John Hoddinott's father and grandfather before him joined the Hampshire Constabulary. However, John decided to make a start in the Metropolitan Police and served in that force until he was appointed Assistant Chief Constable in Surrey. He came home to Hampshire in 1983 as the Deputy Chief Constable before moving up to head the force in 1988. He was a prominent Chief Constable who in 1995 was the Association of Chief Police Officers' President. He played a major role in the development of Automatic Fingerprint Recognition, and led the inquiry into security after the bombing of the Grand Hotel in Brighton.

He was awarded the CBE in 1994 and in 1998 he was knighted. He retired in 1999. Sir John tragically died in 2001 at the age of 56 leaving a widow Lady Avril and two daughters, Rebecca and Louise.

Paul KERNAGHAN (1999-) Whilst at Queen's University, Belfast, he served in the Ulster Defence Regiment, being commissioned in 1976. He joined the Royal Ulster Constabulary in 1978 before transferring as a Superintendent to the West Midlands Force. In 1994 he attended the Senior Command Course and in 1995 he was appointed Assistant Chief Constable in North Yorkshire. In 1996 he was designated Deputy Chief Constable and in 1999 he took over as Chief Constable of Hampshire Constabulary.

**PORTSMOUTH**

The first paid and full-time police force in the city (then a Borough) of Portsmouth was sworn in before the Lord Mayor on 18 March 1836. At the beginning the officers did not even possess uniforms. It was not until later that year that some of the officers were given frock coats, top hats, great coats, capes and belts.

On 11 December 1839 the Council agreed that the force should consist of one superintendent, three inspectors, three sub-inspectors and 24 constables. The starting wage for a constable at that time was just 17 shillings per week, whilst the Superintendent earned £100 per year.

From its inception until its amalgamation with the Hampshire Force, Portsmouth Police had only eight Chief Constables, the first person to carry such a title being appointed in 1875. Prior to that the force had been headed by a Superintendent, the first of whom was Captain Robert Elliott, a former soldier who served with the 82nd Regiment of Foot.

The Chief Constables and their terms of office were:

| James JERVIS | 1875 - 1880 | Thomas DAVIES | 1907 - 1940 |
| A.W. COSSER | 1880 - 1893 | Arthur Charles WEST | 1940 - 1958 |
| H.B. Le MESURIER | 1893 - 1898 | William Newrick WILSON | 1958 - 1964 |
| Arthur T. PRICKETT | 1898 - 1907 | Owen FLYNN | 1964 - 1967 |

When the force amalgamated it consisted of 550 officers made up as follows:

| | | | |
|---|---|---|---|
| Chief Constable | 1 | Sergeants | 76 |
| ACC | 1 | Constables | 413 |
| Superintendent Class | 7 | Woman Police Inspector | 1 |
| Chief Inspectors | 4 | Women Police Sergeant | 3 |
| Inspectors | 24 | Women Police Constables | 20 |

Chief Constable Flynn retired on amalgamation, as the City Force was absorbed into Hampshire and headed by a Chief Superintendent, Portsea Island. Cosham Police Station became part of the Havant Division.

## SOUTHAMPTON

Southampton Police came into being in 1836, seven years after the formation of the Metropolitan Police, and one year after the passing of the Municipal Corporation Act requiring provincial boroughs to organise police forces.

As happened in many places, an inspector was 'borrowed' from the London Force to help organise the new force. The officer in question was John Thomas Enright, an Inspector from A Division Metropolitan Police. It was not until 31 years later, the year before his retirement, that he took on the title of High (or Head) Constable.

At a meeting of the Watch Committee on 18 January 1836 it was decided that the force should consist of one inspector paid 30 shillings a week, one first sergeant paid 21 shillings, a second sergeant paid 20 shillings and 22 constables receiving the modest amount of 16 shillings a week but with two shillings a week deducted towards their uniform. Inspector Enright was appointed at a salary of £150 a year.

From its inception until its amalgamation with the Hampshire Force, Southampton Police had ten Chief Constables, although that title was not assumed until 1867.

The Chief Constables and their terms of office were:

| | | | |
|---|---|---|---|
| John T. ENRIGHT | 1836 - 1868 | John Thomas McCORMAC | 1926 - 1940 |
| Thomas BREARY | 1868 - 1889 | Herbert Clifford ALLEN | 1940 - 1941 |
| Philip Steven CLAY | 1889 - 1892 | Frederick Thomas TARRY | 1941 - 1946 |
| William BERRY | 1892 - 1907 | Charles George BOX | 1947 - 1960 |
| William Edward JONES | 1907 - 1926 | Alfred Thomas CULLEN | 1960 - 1967 |

Chief Constable Thomas Breary, who was born in Spofforth, Yorkshire, commenced his policing career in the Metropolitan Police, before moving on to Bedfordshire, City of London Police, and Buckinghamshire Police. He finally arrived in Southampton on 20 January 1868 and served until his retirement on 6 May 1889.

William Edward Jones, born in Swansea in 1907, previously served with both Stockton and Bradford Police before taking over in Southampton. He died in office on 29 April 1926.

When the force amalgamated it consisted of 499 officers made up as follows:

| | | | |
|---|---|---|---|
| Chief Constable | 1 | Sergeants | 61 |
| ACC | 1 | Constables | 384 |
| Superintendent Class I | 1 | Woman Police Inspector | 1 |
| Superintendent Class II | 6 | Woman Police Sergeant | 1 |
| Chief Inspectors | 3 | Women Police Constables | 16 |
| Inspectors | 24 | | |

Although it covered a much larger geographical area than Portsmouth, fewer officers policed it. Alfred Cullen retired at the time of amalgamation and the city Force became the Southampton Division of the Hampshire Force under the command of a Chief Superintendent.

## ISLE OF WIGHT

The first Police Force on the Isle of Wight was the Newport Borough Police, which was formed in 1837. It was some years before the second Borough Force was formed. In 1869 Ryde set its own force up and a picture of the force is included in the book.

In 1889 Newport Borough Force became part of the newly formed Isle of Wight Constabulary. Ryde did not become part of the Isle of Wight until 1922. In 1943 the Isle of Wight Constabulary became part of the Hampshire Joint Police Force.

## OTHER FORCES

Few records remain of the Andover, Lymington, Basingstoke or Romsey Borough Forces. However, there is a picture showing the Basingstoke Force at the time of amalgamation in 1889, as well as a photograph of the original Basingstoke Police Station.

## TRANSPORT

One theme running through the book is that of transport. The book shows the evolution from horse and cart through to the high performance Volvo T5 that is used today.

One mode of transport that has endured over the years has been the humble pedal cycle and you will find that it is still used today by some officers as the most effective means of getting from one point to another whilst maintaining contact with the public.

In the early years of the 20th century the county force relied increasingly on pedal cycles in their daily work. In 1902 a constable was commended for his 'smartness in hiring a bicycle and following a motorcar which was being driven furiously at Worthy, resulting in his overtaking it in Winchester'. By 1904 constables were paid £2 per annum bicycle allowance. It was not until 1925 that Ford motorcars replaced the horse and cart. In 1926 solo motorcycles were introduced for patrol duties, followed in 1931 by a motorcycle combination.

Increase in the public use of motor vehicles saw the police drivers recognised as traffic officers. However, it was not until 1 July 1945 that Hampshire Constabulary set up a traffic and communications department in Winchester, intended to co-ordinate traffic problems, accident prevention and motor patrols.

The establishment of such a department was necessary due to the growing weight and complexity of motor traffic. Society was becoming more and more mobile and the police had to adapt its methods and equipment accordingly.

In 1967 we saw the first of the 'panda' cars in the force, when five Austin Minis were purchased for use in Basingstoke.

Other forms of transport include the various police launches that have been used both by Hampshire and the Borough Forces. More recently the Hampshire Force has created an Air Support Unit, now on its third generation of aircraft, which houses state of the art equipment to assist with policing the two counties.

## WORLD WARS

The two World Wars brought tragic losses to the police forces within Hampshire and the Isle of Wight. During the Great War, 1914-1918, 21 officers from the Hampshire Force alone were killed on active service.

During the Second World War, 1939-1945, 425 officers served in the armed forces. Of these 14 were killed in action, 14 were wounded and three were taken prisoner. Many officers received war and campaign medals, and several received awards for bravery, gallantry and distinguished service.

War Reservists and Special Constables aided those officers who remained in the police service. Particularly hard hit during the blitz were Portsmouth and Southampton officers, with eight from Portsmouth and three from Southampton losing their lives, whilst 20 were injured. Nine officers received awards for bravery during the raids, the most notable being Goronwy Evans GM, who is featured in this book.

The Southampton Civic Centre, which housed the Central Police Station, was the target of many German raids during the Second World War. On 29 November 1940 one bomb landed on the old 'dung heap' behind the stable building, killing the Chief's driver, PC 66 Frederick Tupper.

## TECHNOLOGY

As technology develops, so the police service has had to adapt and change its equipment and procedures. In early times the mode of communication on the beat was what was known as 'making a point'. Constables met their sergeants and inspectors at pre-ordained locations and times. Officers were also equipped with whistles to summon assistance.

The introduction of the Radio Car meant that, for the first time, emergencies could be passed to police officers by radio and their response could be much quicker. Officers on foot still relied on calling in for 'jobs' at police telephone points, some of which are illustrated in the book.

Eventually in the 1960s the era of the personal radio arrived. Although at first the radio was in two parts — a transmitter and a receiver — equipment has gradually become more sophisticated and now officers are in touch with their colleagues at all times and in all of the furthest reaches of the two counties.

## FINAL AMALGAMATION

On 1 April 1967 the last of the independent city forces in Southampton and Portsmouth joined the rest of the County Police Force, and the Hampshire Constabulary was born. Douglas Osmond OBE became the first Chief Constable of the truly united force covering both Hampshire and the Isle of Wight.

In 1974 local government changes resulted in the loss of some 55 officers to Dorset when the county boundary was changed and Christchurch became part of Dorset.

The current Hampshire Constabulary has an establishment of 3,510 police officers who are supported by about 1,500 civilian colleagues. As years have passed many of the jobs that were initially undertaken by police officers are now performed by support staff.

The days of typewriters and carbon paper now belong to the past as modern computers enable swift production of reports and forms.

Police equipment and uniform have also developed over the years; you can see the development of uniform over the 160 years that the force has been in existence. Police officers now routinely carry CS spray, rigid handcuffs and the metal expandable truncheon, known as the ASP.

## HAMPSHIRE CONSTABULARY HISTORY SOCIETY

Hampshire Constabulary History Society was formed in February 1986 with the aim of stimulating and maintaining interest in the history of the various forces that make up the current Hampshire Constabulary. The society maintains a force museum at Netley and has a large collection of photographs, uniforms, equipment and other artefacts. Many items are rescued from police stations, but a large number of acquisitions come from generous donations from former officers or their families.

Various members, both serving and retired, have contributed photographs of themselves and most of the current committee appear in the book.

This book includes just a small fraction of the many photographs of policing in Hampshire and the Isle of Wight. It has been made possible by the hard work of the members of the society. The society is in the process of continuing a project started by ex-sergeant Geoff Knott to catalogue the photographs and identify people, places and events.

It is inevitable that the book will not be able to illustrate every aspect of policing history within the Force over the years. The Force does, however, possess an enormous collection of photographs and documents and it is hoped that, in time, when the collection has been catalogued, a further book may be published.

The authors would like to acknowledge the work done by Ian Watt and his excellent book, *A History of the Hampshire and Isle of Wight Constabulary 1839-1966*. Many of the details relating to past chief constables have been drawn from that source. We have also drawn on information contained in histories of the two city forces: *A History of the Police of Portsmouth*, one of the Portsmouth Papers series and compiled by ex-Inspector Jim Cramer, and *A History of the Southampton City Police*, produced by Chief Constable Alfie Cullen on amalgamation in 1967, both provided invaluable information.

# THE PLATES

1 Toll House, Buckland, Lymington. Lymington Borough Police Force, comprising a town sergeant and one constable, existed from 1836 until 1852. On joining with the Hampshire Constabulary in 1853, its first station was at Buckland, adjacent to the *Crown Inn* and behind the tollhouse. In 1866 it was replaced by the Queen Anne building in Gosport Street, Lymington. A new police station was erected in 1952 to cater for the immense changes in the Hythe and Lymington areas. The Toll House was operated by the constables. It still stands in the grounds of the *Crown Inn*.

2 County Headquarters of the Hampshire Constabulary, built in 1847 and situated next to Winchester County Prison. Former officers may have vivid memories of their early training in this building before the introduction in the 1940s of regional training centres. These buildings were demolished in 1966 to make way for the present County HQ building. This picture was taken between 1850 and 1865 when the officers wore 'stove pipe hats' rather than the now traditional helmet.

**3** The original Whitchurch Police Station, built in 1862, still standing but now a private house. A new station was built in Dances Close in the 1970s.

**4** P.C. James Hibberd, born in 1848, who served from 1870 to 1898 in Hampshire Constabulary. A labourer prior to joining, he lived near Salisbury. During his career he served at South Warnborough, Odiham, Lymington, Lyndhurst, Hollybourne, Bournemouth, Cosham, Michelmersh, Hardway, Botley, Basingstoke, Alton, Aldershot and Farley Mount. He retired as a First Class Sergeant in 1898. The only blot on his copybook was when in 1872 he was found the worse for drink at Lyndhurst Police Station and fined five shillings. The photograph was taken in the 1870s.

HANTS CONSTABULARY.
WANTED
INTELLIGENT AND ACTIVE
YOUNG MEN
PAY on joining 19s. 10d. per week
UNIFORM AND AN ALLOWANCE FOR BOOTS, WITH PROSPECT OF QUICK PROMOTION.
Soldiers belonging to the Army Reserve are eligible.
☞ Application to be made in Candidate's own Handwriting to
THE CHIEF CONSTABLE OF HAMPSHIRE,
1st May, 1876. WEST HILL, WINCHESTER.
WARREN, TYP. WINTON.

**5** The first Bournemouth Police Station, Oxford Road (now Madeira Road), photographed in 1875, showing the entire division, Sgt. Catchlove and three constables. Sergeant Catchlove joined the force in 1854 and went on to become a Second Class Superintendent before he retired in 1891. By 1948 the borough had grown in size and it became a borough police force in its own right, at a time when no fewer than 45 other borough forces had been abolished.

**6** Police recruiting poster from 1876. How times have changed! The advert was exclusively for men. Today, women officers account for 23 per cent of Hampshire Constabulary. The poster mentions quick promotion as an incentive; however, what it does not mention is that drunkenness and poor performance, linked to strict discipline, meant that demotion was equally quick, and officers were often promoted and demoted several times.

7 Captain John Henry Forrest, the third Chief Constable of Hampshire. He held office from 1856 until 1891. Before coming to Hampshire he was Chief Constable of Nottingham Police. He had a reputation for being a strict disciplinarian and a martinet. He ran the Hampshire Force with a rod of iron.

8 P.C. 73 George Yeates was appointed on 30 November 1861. He was born in Fordingbridge and before joining the constabulary was a shoemaker. He started his service at Four Posts and in July 1862 he was fined 10 shillings for 'allowing himself to be treated'. As a result he was transferred to Preston Candover. Over the next couple of years he was promoted to Second Class and then First Class Constable. He also served at East Boldre, Cheriton, Alverstoke, Hythe and Gosport. In January 1867 he was fined a week's pay for being drunk and absent from his beat. His records show that he died whilst still serving but there is no record of a date or cause of death.

9 PC 148 Robert Gilbert joined Hampshire Constabulary in July 1857. He served on the Isle of Wight, at Ringwood, Whitchurch, Shirley and several other stations all over Hampshire. In 1871 he was promoted to the rank of sergeant. However, in 1879, as a result of an inspection visit from the Chief Constable, he was demoted to constable. The Chief was concerned at the mess that Sergeant Gilbert had let his police station at Whitchurch get into. The Chief Constable described Sergeant Gilbert's bedroom as 'more like the residence of a dealer in bones and rags'. At the same time he was accused of using 'insulting and provoking language to the officer in charge'. This related to an incident where Inspector Kinshott accused him of being 'more drunk than sober' and 'being unable to read the labels on PC's clothing'. He never did regain his rank and retired as a constable in February 1892. This photograph was probably taken in about 1870.

**10** Superintendent Julius Sillence joined the Hampshire Force at the age of 23 in 1871. A groom by profession, he was appointed Deputy Chief Constable in 1895. He retired on 6 May 1906 after 35 years' service. In 1886, whilst a Superintendent, he was commended for swift and decisive action, making use of the 'wires' to contact the Detective Department of the Metropolitan to seek assistance for the murder of James Parker. The public prosecutor did not want to take the case on and Supt Sillence, with an Inspector Lawler, collected all the evidence. An Albert Brown was convicted of the murder.

**11** Basingstoke Borough Police at the time of their amalgamation in 1889 with Hampshire Constabulary. The dog is a pet. Working police dogs of whatever breed did not appear in Hampshire until the 1950s. Basingstoke Borough Police was formed in 1836. *Back row, left to right*: Sergeant Trodd, PC Mears, PC Astridge and PC Treagus. *Front row, left to right*: PC White, PC Burdon and PC Hibbert.

**12** The old police station in Basingstoke was situated in New Street and erected in 1816; it remained in use as a police station until 1889 when the borough force transferred to the Hampshire Constabulary. In later years it was used as a dwelling until its demolition in 1964. Former officers will remember its replacement, the old Mark Lane Police Station, before that too became inadequate for the fast growing population.

**13** Horse-drawn police prison van, or Black Maria, outside Kingston Prison, Milton Road, Portsmouth in about 1890.

**14** Hampshire Officers illustrating the use of the stocks and whipping post at Odiham, *c.*1905. These stocks can still be seen in Odiham. (Stocks were not used in England after about 1840.) *Left to right*: PC Matthews, PC Davis, PC Butler, PC Open, Sgt Morgan and PC Ward.

**15** Captain Peregrine Fellowes, Chief Constable of the Hampshire Constabulary from 1891 to 1893. Following an illustrious military career, he was selected from 74 other applicants to become Hampshire's Chief Constable, taking up the post in May 1891. Although a strict disciplinarian, he was described as fair to those who made errors of judgement. This was illustrated when he allowed PC Boyde a week's unpaid leave to recapture a prisoner whom through negligence they had allowed to escape. On 2 October 1893 Captain Fellowes was off duty and leaving police HQ Winchester for a day's shooting. Three police officers returning to HQ had formed a chain of sorts across the road in an attempt to stop a runaway horse and trap. Captain Fellowes joined his officers but was caught by the shaft of the trap. He tragically died from his injuries on 30 November 1893. The Chief Constable was buried at West Hill Cemetery, Winchester on 4 December 1893, just a short distance from the accident.

**16** Police Constable 165 Alfred Bramwell joined the Portsmouth force on 29 December 1893 at the age of 25. All Portsmouth officers had photographs like this taken which were attached to their personal records. Born in Buxton, he was a whitesmith by trade and had also served in the South Lancashire Regiment from 1886 until 1893. He retired after 26 years' service with a pension of £165 4s. 8d.

**17** The Band of the Southampton County Borough Police, February 1900. At the beginning band members used their own instruments. However, regular concerts raised sufficient funds so that £500 could be spent on a new set of instruments.

**18** Isle of Wight Police in 1900. The picture is believed to have been taken at Sandown. Notice that the officer third from the left in the 'kepi' has four stripes which denotes the rank of 'Senior Sergeant'. Also note that both sergeants wear their stripes on only one sleeve of their tunics.

**19** Superintendents of Hampshire Constabulary, 1 August 1900. *Back row*: Supt. Courtney; Supt. Jacobs; Supt. Silver; Supt. Griffin; Supt. Hawkins; Supt. King; Supt. Wakeford; Supt. Bowles. *Front row*: Supt. Daniels; Supt. James; Supt. Hack; Supt. Sillence (DCC); Supt. Foster; Supt. Hale; Supt. Payne.

**20** Superintendent Samuel Foster in ceremonial uniform complete with sword. Previously a servant by trade, he joined Hampshire Constabulary on 9 March 1872. He served at Gosport, Upton Grey, Bitterne, East Boldre, Stockbridge, Andover, Ventnor, Ringwood, Sandhurst, Petersfield and finally at Bournemouth. By 1891 he had been promoted to Superintendent, but in 1893 he was reduced to the rank of Inspector for discreditable conduct. However, he again rose to the rank of Superintendent and was still at Bournemouth as a First Class Superintendent when he died on 30 July 1904.

**21** Winchester City officers at the laying of the First Boundary Stone of Greater Winchester, 15 November 1900. The officer on the immediate left foreground is from Hampshire Constabulary, the remainder are from Winchester City. The policeman on the far right is thought to be PC William Theodore Burner of the Winchester City Police. PC Burner joined the Winchester Force on 2 September 1881. He went on to become a sergeant before he was retired as medically unfit in 1909. In 1894, whilst attempting to arrest two burglars in St James Lane, he was badly assaulted and disabled which resulted in six months' sick leave, a commendation and compensation of £3.

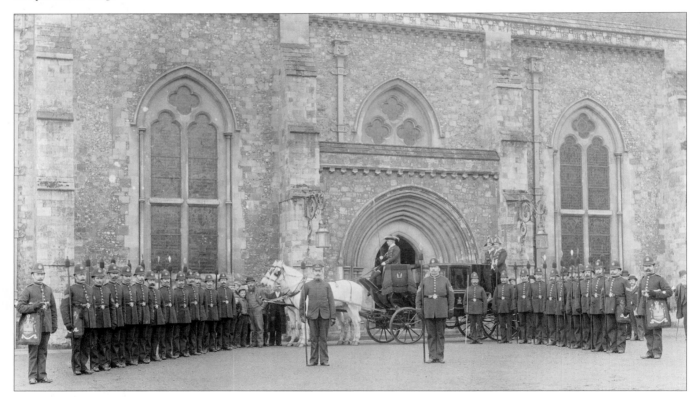

**22** Prior to the advent of the Crown Court system, the highest court within the County was the Assizes held in Hampshire at the Great Court, Winchester. A significant police presence always formed the High Court Judge's escort. This was a ceremonial as well as a security function. The officers on parade outside the Great Court in 1900 are commanded by the Deputy Chief Constable of Hampshire, Julius Sillence (front left in cap).

**23** The picture shows officers in Lyndhurst in the Victorian era.

**24**  A group of Hampshire officers in front of the old Police Headquarters, West Hill, Winchester, *c*.1900. Until the 1950s all Hampshire Constabulary officers were trained in this building before being posted to a station and working the beat. There was little co-ordination of training between different forces at this time; former officers speak of only a very few days spent on any academic work during those early times at Police Headquarters.

**25**  Droxford Police Station was built in 1858 together with the local courthouse. A divisional station in early years, it became a section station for the Meon Valley until 1993, when it was sold. Policing responsibility moved to the officer in charge at the new station at nearby Bishops Waltham. The court was not used after 1986. The picture shows the old station in 1901 with the officer in charge, Sergeant Padwick.

**26**  The Hampshire Constabulary mounted branch in 1901, on a fortnight's course under riding master Parr, RHA, Royal Artillery barracks, Aldershot. (*Left to right*) Sergeant Smith, PC's Hewett, Green, Aylesbury, Stone, Plowman, Miles, and West. The mounted branch remained an important ingredient of the force until its eventual demise in the 1920s when the motorcar began to take over as the preferred method of transport.

**27**  Thomas Clarke joined the Hampshire
Constabulary in 1879 and served at Aldershot,
Freemantle, Shirley, Alton, Sarisbury and Droxford
before resigning in 1883. He left Hampshire
Constabulary on 20 March 1883 and joined the
Southampton Borough Police Force four days later. He
served in the Southampton Force until 1902, working
his way up through the six different classes of Constable
to Third Class Sergeant. The photograph shows
Sergeant Clarke when he was part of the River Police
section in about 1901.

**28**  Winchester City Police Force, taken in 1902 at Abbey
Gardens. The city had its own force from 1832. Its
primary task was to deal with the problems caused by
vagrants within the city. The force remained a separate
entity until it amalgamated with Hampshire in 1943.
*Second row*: far left is PC Wadmore; second from right is
PC Muldawney; *Front row*, third from right is PS Jeliff.

**29**  PC 66 Robert George Poore of the Portsmouth Borough Police. Poore, a labourer, was born on 12 May 1868 in Portsmouth. In 1893, aged 25, he joined the police and at that time was described as 6 ft. 2 ins. tall, with grey eyes, fresh complexion, and light brown hair. His police service was fairly uneventful according to his service record, but he did have his moment of fame long after he retired from the force. On 25 April 1932 one of the most serious robberies committed in Portsmouth took place. A bank clerk and a messenger, ex-PC Poore, were attacked by three men at the junction of Edinburgh Road and Commercial Road. Ex-PC Poore was carrying a bag containing £23,477. The two men were knocked to the floor and the bag snatched from them. The three men ran to a nearby getaway car and drove off. Ex-PC Poore, now 64 years old, chased after the car and jumped on the running board. However he was again struck by the men and fell off into the road, barely conscious. Although the money was never recovered the car was later found in a lock-up in Southsea. As a result three men were arrested and each received long terms of imprisonment and strokes of the cat. Ex-PC Poore was awarded the princely sum of £5 for his bravery by Lloyds Bank. After his retirement PC Poore became a judge at Crufts Dog Show where his speciality was West Highland Terriers.  He died at the ripe old age of 94 in about 1962. The photograph shows PC Poore helping children across Commercial Road, Portsmouth, near the junction with Edinburgh Road. It is thought that the photograph was posed in about 1903.

**30**  PC 66 Robert George Poore of the Portsmouth Borough Police. He joined in 1893 and retired in 1919 with a pension of 33 shillings a week.

**31**  Ryde Borough Police Force, 1903. It was formed in 1869 and did not become part of the Isle of Wight Constabulary until 1922, which then amalgamated with Hampshire in 1943.

**32** The Police Station, Whitehill, with mounted officer and beat officers. Taken from a postcard posted on 18 December 1906. The police station, which was provided by the Army, was erected in 1904. The current Whitehill Police Station stands on the same site.

**33** The Hampshire Police and Fire Brigade at the scene of the Burberry fire, Basingstoke, 1905.

**34** Sergeant 62 William Padwick, a labourer from Houghton, near Stockbridge, joined the Hampshire Force on 23 May 1891. He was promoted to Sergeant in 1900 and then served at Droxford from 1901 until 1911. The horse and cart remained in use until well into the 1920s, particularly in the rural areas. Although a former Division, Droxford remained the section station for the Meon Valley until 1993, supporting former rural beats at Denmead, Hambledon, Exton, Soberton, West Meon, Swanmore, Upham, Bishops Waltham and Wickham.

**35** Witer, a Belgian convict, who escaped from Winchester Prison, between PS Richards and PC Smith at Andover in 1909. He was recaptured in the Leckford-Longstock area and taken to Andover. Sergeant John Richards joined the force on 23 April 1898 and went on to become a Superintendent, receiving a King's Jubilee Medal in 1935.

**36**   A very early (*c.*1906) Road Traffic Accident involving a Daimler motorcar and a cart in St Cross Road, Winchester. Would these tyres pass an MOT test today? The registration 'DU' was issued by the Registration Authority in Coventry between December 1903 and 1919.

**37** P.C. 36 James Hibberd joined the Hampshire Constabulary on 27 August 1904. PC Hibberd was the son of PC James Hibberd (see no.4). During his service he served at Boscombe, Botley, Chief Constable's Office, Aldershot, Bournemouth and Farnborough. He retired as an Inspector in January 1937. This photo was taken at Winchester in 1907.

**38** PC 194 William Henry Gosling joined the Portsmouth Borough Police on 1 September 1908, aged 25 years and 6 months. He was 5 ft. 10½ ins. tall, with brown hair and blue eyes and was born in Wandsworth on 5 October 1882. Before joining he was a Marine. He died in 1958. His pension at that time was £152 2s. 10d. His widow continued to receive a widow's pension until her death on 31 December 1996.

**39** Boscombe Police outing, 3 February 1908.
At this time Bournemouth/ Boscombe was a Division within the Hampshire Force. The sergeant is Bill Deacon who retired as the Bournemouth Divisional Superintendent in 1938. With the reins is Charlie Pounds, believed to be the founder of Royal Blue Shamrock Rambler Coaches. 'Happy Days of Yesteryear!'

**40** Basingstoke Division, 1910 at the Mark Lane Police Station, Basingstoke. This police station was to remain in use for over 50 more years. Former officers will remember its parquet floors that were polished nightly by the station duty officer.

**41** D Division Officers photographed at the rear of Kingston Cross Police Station in 1910. This station was built in 1896 in London Road, opposite the junction with Kingston Crescent. It closed in 1963 when the new police station in Kingston Crescent was opened.

**42** Winton Sub-Division, Bournemouth, 1912. PC Malcolm McCallum (*seated extreme right*) joined the Constabulary in 1907 at the age of 17, but falsely gave his age as 21 to get in. This discrepancy was not officially noticed until 1943 by which time he was a Superintendent based at Aldershot. During the First World War he left the police service to serve in the army, fighting in France, rising to the rank of Major in the Indian Army. Major McCallum rejoined the force in 1921 and served until May 1950. In 1927 he was an Inspector, serving in the CID at Bournemouth, earning £310 per annum. In 1949 as a Superintendent he was earning £850 per annum. He was awarded the MBE in June 1949. Following retirement he worked as an advisor on security to firms such as Timothy Whites. He died in 1958.

**43** PC 439 Stephen Hollett wearing uniform for the first time after his recruit course at H.Q. in August 1913. Born near Dover in Kent, he was a gardener before joining the Hampshire Force. He later became a sergeant and retired in 1945 with a pension of £248 10s. 11d.

**44** Hampshire Mounted Police, Aldershot - June 1913.
*Back Row*: P.C. Marshall; P.C. Holyome; P.C. Rickman; P.C. Smeeth; P.C. Wigmore; P.C. Creighton; P.C. Herage; P.C. Poling; P.C. Lilywhite;
*Front Row*: P.C. Wilson; P.C. Bunning; P.C. Thornton; Supt. Davis; Captain Caddington RHA; Sgt Pike; P.C. Nicholson; P.C. Clark; P.C. Garrett;
*Seated in front*: P.C. Gibbins; P.C. Goodchild.
It is interesting that at this time the officers still carried swords.

**45** Officers of Romsey Division during the 1914-1918 War. The War would probably have accounted for the presence of the military personnel in the group. Bicycles were still and for many years to come the principal means of transport for the bobby on the beat. Romsey had originally been a borough force in its own right but was amalgamated with Hampshire County Police in 1865.

**46** A Hampshire Constable from the early 1920s. The jacket with white piping was known as the Norfolk jacket. The helmet is of the round-segmented type rather than the familiar 'combed' helmet.

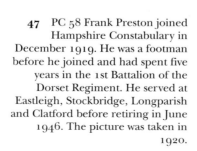

**47** PC 58 Frank Preston joined Hampshire Constabulary in December 1919. He was a footman before he joined and had spent five years in the 1st Battalion of the Dorset Regiment. He served at Eastleigh, Stockbridge, Longparish and Clatford before retiring in June 1946. The picture was taken in 1920.

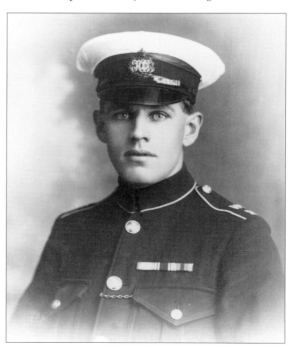

**48** Major St Andrew Bruce Warde, Chief Constable of Hampshire between 1894 and 1928. This picture was taken by PC 53 A.E. Punter in 1922.

**49** PC 145 William Frank Hudd (Mounted Branch) outside an unknown country house somewhere in the Eastleigh area. He joined the Force on 12 March 1920 having previously worked as a groom. He also served with his brother Charles in the 15th Hampshire Carabineer Regiment. His brother also joined the force in 1920.

**50** Hampshire County Police, Winchester Division Football Team, 1925-6.

**51** Portsmouth Borough Police water polo team, 1926, which played in Portsmouth and District Water Polo League Division III.
*Back row*: Arthur Young; Phil Boulter; — ; Albert Cooper; George Roberts; — .
*Front row*: 'Firpo' Ford; PC Larcombe; Jack Shepard; Bob James; 'Long' Johnson.
Arthur Young left Portsmouth in November 1938 to take up the appointment of Chief Constable of Leamington Spa. He was subsequently knighted and, when he finally retired from the police service, he was Commissioner of Police in the City of London.

**52** Hampshire Constabulary Headquarters Staff, March 1929. *Back row*: PC J.W. Hall; PC F. I. Williams; PC A.L. Cooper; PC W.R. Trent; PC W.M. Coombes; PC H.W. Pearce; PC C.J. McCahey. *Front row*: PC G. Hatcher; Inspector F. Osman; Supt R. Knox; Sgt Major B.H. Waters; Sgt A.C. West; PC E.L. Chown.

Sergeant Arthur Charles West went on to become Chief Constable of Portsmouth City Force between 1940 and 1958. Arthur West joined Hampshire on 23 December 1921 and had previously worked as a chauffeur. George Hatcher joined Hampshire on 12 March 1926 and retired as a Chief Superintendent at Havant in 1967. Inspector Frank Osman, who joined Hampshire in July 1912, was appointed Assistant Chief Constable in 1942 before retiring on New Year's Eve 1951. Edward Chown joined on 5 January 1925, retiring as a Superintendent at Andover in 1963.

**53** Judges Escort, Southampton. Chief Constable McCormac is in the carriage. The inscription over the door of the building reads, 'Queen Victoria Jubilee Institute'. John Thomas McCormac was the first Chief Constable of Southampton to have been promoted from within the Force. He was a Superintendent when the previous Chief Constable, William Jones, died in office. He took command as Chief on 1 November 1926. Born in Waterford, Ireland, on 12 January 1900, he retired on 1 April 1940.

**54**   Hampshire Constabulary,
Andover Division.
Winners of the Constabulary Cricket
Competition, 1931.
*Back row*: PC Series; PC Day; PC
Eagle; PC Oliver; PC Eyles.
*Middle row*: PC Radford; PC Preston;
PC Broomfield; PC Noyes; PC
Ballard.
*Front row*: PC Sibbick; PC Old.

**55**   Isle of Wight Constabulary, Ryde Section, 1932.
*Back row*: S. Mariner; T. Denness; G. Thatcher; W. Floyd; C. Lowe.
*Middle row*: J. Barber; F. Rugman; B. Swann; W. Groves; J. Turnbull; T. McVicar.
*Front row*: T. Hodges; Sgt O. Palmer; Insp A. Morrison; Sgt G. Dobson; P. Pullinger.

**56** Winchester City Police mounted branch in the 1930s prior to being disbanded as a result of the advent of motorised transport.

**57** With the passing of the first Road Traffic Act, 1930, forces in England and Wales were required to provide police traffic patrols. These were the first Portsmouth City Police motorcycle combinations. *From left to right*: PC 103 Samuel Luke (rider); the passenger and constable standing next to the machine are unknown. PC Luke, born in Farnborough, joined the Portsmouth Force on 12 January 1926. The gentleman in civilian clothes is the Chief Constable, Thomas Davies. He was Chief Constable from 1907 until 1940. He was 35 years old when he was appointed and promised to serve for at least five years. He stayed for 33! He was previously with Carmarthen and became Chief Constable in Hove. Riding the second machine is PC Ernest Middleton who joined on 25 November 1924. He ended his service as a Temporary Inspector. His passenger, PC George Bleach, joined the force on 22 November 1927. It is believed that this photograph was taken in the yard at the rear of Kingston Cross Police Station. This police station closed in 1963 and the officers moved to the new police station in Kingston Crescent.

**58** The first Portsmouth Police patrol car, a Wolseley Hornet, outside Portsmouth Guildhall in 1934. The Guildhall accommodated police headquarters and also Central Police Station. The man seated behind the wheel is believed to be the Chairman of the Watch Committee. Also in the photograph are (*from left to right*), the Chief Constable, Thomas Davies, PC Ernest Middleton, and PC George Bleach.

**59** Winchester City in the 1930s. Policemen on point duty at the junction of Jewry Street and Southgate Street, looking down towards the Butter Cross. The shopping area has now been pedestrianised and traffic lights control the junction. At this time officers of the old Winchester City force were still policing the city.

**60** The Bournemouth division winning relay team at Fleming Park, Eastleigh 1935.
Sydney Bennett, *far left*, the Andover Superintendent with the winning team of P.C.s S. Vallence, S. Davies, Girvan and Strange. Mr Bennett was Superintendent in Bournemouth in 1948 when Bournemouth became a separate Police Force. He became the new Bournemouth Police Chief Constable.

**61** Rattenbury Murder.
In May 1935 Mrs Alma Rattenbury, 38 years, and her chauffeur, George Stoner, 18 years, were on trial accused of murdering Mr Rattenbury, 68 years. The two officers shown are PC Arthur Bagwell (*left*) and Inspector William J. Mills (*right*) leaving the Old Bailey. PC Bagwell had been the first on the scene of the murder in Bournemouth at about 2a.m. on 25 March 1935 and he was joined shortly afterwards by Inspector Mills, the only uniformed Inspector involved in the case. The murder became headline news because Mrs Rattenbury and Stoner were lovers. Mrs Rattenbury was acquitted and Stoner was sentenced to death, although the sentence was later commuted to life imprisonment.

**62** Southampton Borough Police Horse 'Warrior' leading the Church Parade on 11 August 1935. Warrior had served in the Great War from 1914 to 1918 through the retreat from Mons and was wounded by shrapnel at Aisnes. He then spent 16 years with Southampton Police. The Hampshire History Society still has one of Warrior's hooves in the force museum.

**63** Southampton Police Band at the Southampton Civic Centre in 1937. The band was reckoned to be a first-class military band. It used to play regularly on a bandstand in Palmerston Park. The bandstand exists today, but is now in the park in Leigh Road, Eastleigh. In the front centre is Chief Constable J.T. McCormac. On his left is his son Sergeant Jack McCormac. Another family connection is the Bandleader, Mr Muddiman, seated to the right of the Chief Constable. His son Frank Muddiman stands in the third row, second from the left. Fifth from the left in the same row is Harold Well.

**64** Prior to 18 August 1941, the Chief Constable of Portsmouth was also responsible for the Portsmouth City Police Fire Brigade. All police officers were trained fire fighters. In this photograph the fire engine, based at Cosham Police Station, is being driven south along Cosham High Street by PC Bill Shepard. Sergeant Arthur is the passenger. The other passenger is not known. It is believed that the photo was taken in 1938. Note the tram lines on the road, although trolley buses had replaced trams in Portsmouth by 1936.

**65** Southampton Chief Constable Frederick Tarry inspecting the Women's Auxiliary Police Corps with a senior WAPC officer. Frederick Tarry started his career with Brighton Police in 1919. In 1931 he moved to Exeter City before taking over as Chief Constable of Southampton on 30 September 1941. During his military service in the Great War he was awarded for Gallantry in the Field (1917) and in the same year was Mentioned in Despatches.

**66** Southampton Borough mobile canteen, 1941, during the Second World War. Extreme right is PC Eric Coleman, who retired as Chief Superintendent at Southampton Central. The Sergeant on the left is Bert Adams who retired as a Detective Superintendent.

**67** Portsmouth City Police, mobile canteen. The picture was taken during the Second World War. The female in the canteen would have been a member of the Women's Auxiliary Police Corps. You will see that the offside headlamp is covered and the extremities of the vehicle are painted in white to aid visibility in black-out conditions.

**68**  PC Goronwy Evans GM. Portsmouth City. Born in Wales in 1918, Goronwy joined the Portsmouth City Police in 1936 as a Boy Fireman. Two years later he became a constable and was posted to Southsea, and two more years later the city was a target for the German air raids of the Blitz. The death and destruction caused by the Luftwaffe became a familiar sight to the officers. On 10 March 1941 Goronwy was patrolling in Elm Grove when a bomb landed and set fire to buildings. Goronwy noticed that next to the burning building was a nursing home, which had not been evacuated. With total disregard for his own safety he entered the burning building to tackle the fire. Twice fumes overcame him, but after treatment he returned to tackle the blaze. In recognition of his bravery he was awarded the George Medal for gallantry by the King. He continued to serve until 1968. He was the only member of the Portsmouth City Police to win the George Medal.

**69**  Hampshire PC 415 Charles Hellard, who joined Hampshire in 1935, making enquiries at a local farm in the 1940s.

**70**  W. G. Stratton, Head Constable of Winchester City Police. William Stratton was with the Winchester force for over 40 years, 17 as Head Constable. He retired in 1942 and died in Winchester in 1954 at the age of 72. During his career he was commended on more than one occasion. In one incident of note a fellow officer had been shot and PC Stratton overpowered and disarmed the offender. Winchester City was the first Police Force in Hampshire, formed in 1832, principally to suppress vagrancy in the city. Although working in close liaison with its larger county neighbours, it retained its own identity until as late as 1943, when legislation required amalgamation with Hampshire Constabulary.

**71**  Members of the successful Portsmouth City Police Rifle Club, *c.*1940.
*Back row*: War Reserve (name not known); PC 313 Norman Johns; PC 127 Gilbert Sturgess; PC Nicholas; *Front row*: PC 199 'Tom' Sidney Weston (team captain); Inspector Powell; PC 128 Noel Kirkby.
As these officers were all skilled marksmen, they were frequently employed on guard or protection duties during the Second World War, when an armed officer was required.

**72**  Roy William Clarke was a Police Messenger in Southampton before joining HM Forces in 1943. The Police Messengers were formed after the outbreak of the war because large numbers of young officers joined the services. At the same time the Women's Auxiliary Police Corps and the Police War Reserve were also formed. The Messenger Service evolved after the war into the Police Cadets. Roy went on to join the Southampton and Hampshire forces. His grandfather is shown in photograph 27.

**73** Southampton Borough Police Civil Defence Training, 1943. The officers include a War Reserve constable, designated by a WR on his collar. He is the third from the left.

**74** PC 147 Charles Bodger and WPC 8 Barbara Ann Williams crewing the Police Radio car in 1943, in High Street, Southampton. PC Bodger, who joined the force on 24 November 1939, was responsible for the illuminated roll of honour for officers who died during the war. It took PC Bodger two and a half years of spare time to draw the roll of honour. A copy of it now hangs at the Hampshire Training School at Netley (see no,186). PC Bodger later joined the Bournemouth Police.

**75** Southampton Borough. Police Constable Charles Bodger at a street pillar in 1943.

**76**  WPC 8 Barbara Ann Williams at Southampton Police Headquarters telephone switchboard in 1944.

**77**  Arthur Charles West, Chief Constable of Portsmouth City Police from 1940 until 1958. Mr. West joined the Hampshire Constabulary in 1921 and served in all ranks at various stations, including Bournemouth, Andover and Fareham. Announcing his appointment as Chief Constable in General Orders, the then Chief Constable of Hampshire, Major Cockburn, said that the Superintendent's achievement reflected great credit on himself and the Hampshire Constabulary as a whole. Mr West left Portsmouth in 1958 to take up the post of Chief Officer with the British Transport Commission Police.

**78**  F. T. Tarry, CB, CBE, Chief Constable of Southampton City Police, 1941 to 1946. In June 1941 Mr Tarry was awarded the King's Police Medal. In 1946 he was made a CBE. Mr Tarry left the force to become one of His Majesty's Inspectors of Constabulary.

**79** Southampton Police launch *Versatile* at Woolston near the Floating Bridge.

**80** Law Sunday, The Castle, Winchester. There are both Winchester City and Hampshire officers taking part in the parade, which must have taken place during the time of the Joint police force, between 1942 and 1947.

**81** Hampshire Constabulary motorcyclists, taken at Winchester in 1948. Traffic Parades such as this took place at Peninsular Barracks in Winchester. The officers are all riding Triumph 498 cc Speed Twin motorcycles, the first vertical twin cylinder motorcycles. *Fifth from left* is PC Frank Green; *second from right* is PC 471 Frank Hunter.

**82** 'A' Division (Civic Centre), Southampton City Police Control Room in about 1949. *Front right*, WPC 7 Gladys Hobbs; *back right*, Pat Rogers; *front left*, PC Palmer; *back left*, PC 230 Sam Brookes. PC Brookes, born in Montevideo, joined the Southampton Force in 1937 and during the war served with the Royal Artillery as a Lance Bombardier. During his military service he was wounded by shrapnel in Italy.

**83**  Animal welfare? Just another job for the man on the beat and an interested crowd has gathered to watch. A swan has lost its way back to Canoe Lake. The unknown constable on foot is from Southsea Police Station (note divisional letter C on his epaulette). He is wearing a closed neck tunic, which dates the photo to about 1950. The back-up police car is a Riley 2 litre driven by PC Len Hoad. This was before blue flashing lights and sirens. The car is equipped with a black loudspeaker for public address, a chrome bell and a lamp with the letter P on the lens. PC Hoad joined Portsmouth City on 3 September 1941, retiring as a sergeant. During the war he served with the Royal Marines, receiving the France and Germany Star, the Defence Medal and War Medal.

**84** Taken in the early 1950s, this Wolseley 12/48 Hampshire County police car is driven by PC Ken Piper with his observer PC George Kirby. PC Piper joined the force in June 1939, left in 1942 to fight in the Second World War and rejoined in 1945. He retired in 1965. PC Kirby came to Hampshire having previously served with the Winchester City Force. He retired as an Information Room Sergeant in 1967.

**85** Portsmouth City Police Headquarters, Queens Crescent, Southsea, *c*.1952. These premises were built for the Brickwood family, local brewers, as a country house within the town. It was originally named Branscombe House which was changed to Byculla House when it became a private school from 1918 to 1939. It was taken over by the police after Portsmouth Guildhall was destroyed by enemy bombing in 1942. It remained police accommodation until the late 1970s when the last officers moved into the new Divisional HQ at Kingston Crescent. In addition to being the training school, the police vehicle workshops were also situated in the grounds.

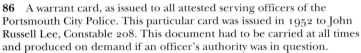

**86**   A warrant card, as issued to all attested serving officers of the Portsmouth City Police. This particular card was issued in 1952 to John Russell Lee, Constable 208. This document had to be carried at all times and produced on demand if an officer's authority was in question.

**87**   Police Constable 208 John Russell Lee, Portsmouth City Police, 1954. The officer is wearing a duty overcoat of that period with a whistle chain. The letter B denotes his division and is worn above his warrant number on the epaulette of the coat. This photograph was taken by Special Sergeant Birdsey, a professional photographer, trading as USA Studios, whose premises were close to Fratton Police Station.

**88**   Special Constables Blackmore, unknown, Humphries, Sid Butler, Harrison, Special Inspector Frank Simpson and Special Sergeant Vince form the Mayor's Escort at the old Andover Council in 1955.

**89** Hampshire Police Cadets. Prior to the Second World War, young men began to be employed in stations as boy clerks. In the early 1950s their role changed to that of a police cadet with a gradual introduction to police work. By the 1970s Police Cadet Training at the Priory, Bishops Waltham ensured a properly structured training programme for potential entry as constables. The photograph is of a training course at Police Headquarters, Winchester in 1955.

*Back Row L to R*: Cadets E. Baldrey; M. Simmonds; I. Hamilton; C. Goddard; Dennis Meadus; Dave Burnett; N. Langdon; J. Keates; M. Pike; J. Wareham; L. Hoare.

*Front Row L to R*: G. Collins; J. Pittard; A. Clarke: Chief Inspector Bond; Sgt Mason; Cadets G. Kemp; Colin Peake; A. J. Clark.

Colin Peake, a member of the Hampshire Constabulary History Society, retired in 1988 as an Inspector. Colin served as both a sergeant and an Inspector in the Training School, initially at Queens Crescent in Portsmouth and then at Bishops Waltham.

**90** PC James Dolan was the village police officer at Weyhill. On 2 December 1956 he tried to stop a car outside his cottage, mistakenly believing it to be stolen. The driver failed to see him in the darkness and the collision threw PC Dolan into the path of another car and he was killed instantly.

The officers in the picture are, nearest to the camera, from front to back, PC Taffy Locke, PC Bob Cameron, PC J. Stratton. On the other side are PC D. Wren, PC D. Wilmott and PC L. Carpenter.

**91**  Hampshire Constabulary patrol motorcycle being ridden by Sergeant Bill Elms who retired as Chief Superintendent in charge of the Traffic Division in 1973. William Elms joined Hampshire Constabulary in 1941 and also served in HM Forces from 1942 to 1945. The picture was taken in about 1957.

**92**  Richard Dawney Lemon, Chief Constable of Hampshire from 1942 to 1962. Mr Lemon was educated at Uppingham and Sandhurst. He served in the Metropolitan, Leicestershire, and Yorkshire Police prior to arriving in Hampshire. The police forces of Winchester and the Isle of Wight merged with the Hampshire Constabulary in 1943 and Mr Lemon was appointed Chief Constable of the joint force. Mr Lemon left Hampshire in 1962 to take command of the Kent force.

**93**  Hampshire Constabulary Traffic Division, at the Peninsular Barracks, Winchester in 1949. Cars are all Wolseley 12/48s. The officer leading the parade is Superintendent Albert Henry Wright, who retired in 1952 after 29 years' service.

**94** Southampton Borough dog section. Police dogs were introduced into Southampton in 1953. Furthest from the camera is PC 209 John William Ryles, who was the first Southampton Borough dog handler, with his Alsatian Mountbrowne Quaker. A professional footballer, he was born in Doncaster. He joined Southampton force on 9 May 1930. The second officer is possibly PC Ron French. By 1966 the force had four dog handlers and dogs. Inspecting are, *from left to right,* Superintendent Alfie Cullen (later Chief Constable), Chief Constable Charles Box and Her Majesty's Chief Inspector of Constabulary, Sir William Johnson. Sir William Johnson joined Portsmouth Borough in 1920, before transferring in 1932 to take up post as Chief Constable of Plymouth. Charles George Box was Chief Constable of Southampton from 1947 to 1960, having previously been the Chief Constable of Great Yarmouth.

**95** Police Officers on a training course at Winchester Headquarters in the late 1950s. The Chief Inspector is Jack Bond. Also present are Sergeants Dean and Fielder and constables include Titheridge, Allan, Buckley, Board, Benson, Barnard, Painter and Ellison.
Alan Barnard, now retired, was a founding member of the Hampshire Constabulary History Society and is currently its treasurer.

**96** PC 327 Frank Eames of Southampton City Police at a police point. Before joining the actual police he had been a Police War Reserve. For many years this was the only contact that an officer had with the station. The police boxes and telephones would gradually disappear with the advent of personal radios.

**97**   Cadets at Southampton, Hulse Road. Far left is Fred Emery. He went on to become a Traffic Motor Cyclist at Bitterne until his retirement. He then went on to work in the ADP Department processing photographs from speed cameras. Third from the left is Roger Berry. Fifth from the left is Ron Sayers, and sixth from left is Terry Burden. Ninth from the left is Howard Willis. Howard was an area car driver and Local Intelligence Officer at Shirley as well as the Football Liaison officer with Southampton Football Club. He still works for the Force, operating the CCTV at Southampton Football Club home matches as well as being one of the Coroner's Officers at Civic Centre Police Station. Tenth from left is Keith White who later became a Detective Chief Inspector. Eleventh from left is Dudley Osmond who served for over thirty years before becoming a handwriting expert for the force as a civilian. He died in 2000. The furthest right is Nigel Butt. Other cadets pictured include Maurice House and John Robins. The sergeant is Peter Turner.

**98**   Southampton Police First Aid Team, 1960.
*Back row*: PC K. Osborne; PC Ivan Leigh; PC D. Edwards.
*Front row*: PC C. Nicholson; Sgt Ellis Rimmer; Chief Constable A. T. Cullen MBE; Insp V. White; Sgt R. Cook.
Sgt Rimmer went on to become the Chief Inspector in charge of Shirley Police Station at the time of amalgamation with Hampshire. Born in Skelmersdale, he had previously been a Sergeant in the Manchester Regiment.

**99** Annual inspection of Portsmouth City Police *c.*1960 by Her Majesty's Inspector of Constabulary, Sir William Clarence Johnson. Sir William started his police career as a constable in Portsmouth. The whole force was on parade in Connaught Drill Hall. Sir William, accompanied by Chief Constable, William N. Wilson, is seen here presenting Good Conduct and Long Service Medals to (*left to right*) Detective Inspector Arthur Richards, Sergeant Don Walters, PC Dennis Bell and Sergeant Charlie Vacher. In the background is Superintendent A. V. Organ (*extreme left*). PC Ray Jones is seen between Bell and Vacher. PC Bernard 'Polly' Parrott is on the extreme right.

**100** Police Constable 241 John 'Tolch' Tolcher, the first dog handler in Portsmouth City Police. He joined in June 1946 after wartime service in the army. He served at Kingston before starting the first dog section in 1956 when he transferred to Portsmouth City HQ. When he retired in March 1971 he was serving at Cosham. PC Tolcher's first dog was the jet black Mountbrowne Ingot (*right*). They worked as a team for almost six years. In 1958 they were lent to the Hampshire Force to track a murderer on the Isle of Wight, earning the thanks of Hampshire's Chief Constable. John and Ingot were responsible for more than a score of arrests and the recovery of a large amount of stolen property. PC Tolcher was commended in 1968 for his courage and restraint in arresting a man armed with a revolver. John died on 5 February 2001. When Ingot retired he paraded wearing boots on his rear paws because of his partial paralysis. The other dog in the picture is Rex (*left*).

**101** PC John Wavell with a
Triumph police motorcycle, possibly
in the 1960s. He joined Hampshire
in 1951 and retired as a sergeant on
the Mobile section in 1982.

**102** Two officers riding Lambretta
scooters from the old Police
Headquarters in Winchester. The
picture was taken in the early 1960s.
The helmet badge is that of the
Hampshire and Isle of Wight
Constabulary.

103    Hampshire Police Officer 66 in about 1962/3 demonstrating mobile communications.

**104** PC 195 Laurie Peake at Petersfield Police Station in 1963 with an Austin A110 patrol car. Laurie recalls one occasion in March 1964 on patrol on the A3 in the Petersfield area when he saw a large multi-coloured lorry travelling towards Portsmouth which he wished to stop. The driver was of a very dark complexion and was wearing a straw boater hat. Laurie was not in a position to stop the vehicle but did manage to stop it later in the day when the lorry was travelling north on the same stretch of road. This time the driver was a white man, but sitting in the passenger seat was a chimpanzee wearing a straw boater. To this day Laurie is puzzled at the thought of the chimp driving. The lorry belonged to Billy Smart's circus.

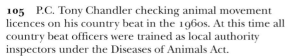

**105** P.C. Tony Chandler checking animal movement licences on his country beat in the 1960s. At this time all country beat officers were trained as local authority inspectors under the Diseases of Animals Act.

**106** Two women police officers of the Hampshire Constabulary outside the Broadway Police Station beneath the Guildhall, Winchester, before a new police station was built at North Walls, Winchester, in the early '60s. Although women police served in Portsmouth and Southampton from 1919, the Hampshire Constabulary did not introduce women officers until the advent of the Second World War.

**107** Hampshire Constabulary control room in the old Police Headquarters building. On the left is PC George Williams. He joined Hampshire in 1949, retiring in 1978, but stayed on in the same role as a civilian in the Personnel Department. In 1977 he was one of the officers who received the present Queen's Jubilee Medal.

**108** Southampton Chief Constable Alfred Cullen inspecting the Traffic Department. He joined Southampton as a constable on 18 July 1930 and worked his way through the ranks to become Chief Constable on 1 April 1960. He remained in post until Southampton amalgamated with Hampshire in 1967 when he retired. The officer being inspected is PC 255 Norman Chalk, previously a professional footballer before he joined the Southampton force in 1939. During the war he served three years with the Royal Corps of Signals as a Lance Corporal. He rejoined the force in 1946 as a Traffic officer.

**109** Southampton Borough Police Traffic Department on parade at the rear of Hulse Road. Sir Charles Cunningham from the Home Office opened the premises in Hulse Road on 20 March 1959. The building housed the traffic garage seen here as well as being the force's Training Headquarters and hostel. You will see that the traffic drivers wore boots with gaiters. Second from the left is PC 72 Fred Cleverly who went on to become the Traffic Chief Inspector at Basingstoke.

**110** HRH The Duke of Edinburgh meeting Chief Constable Cullen, Southampton Borough Police on a Royal Visit.

**111** Southampton City dog handlers, PC Eric Fielder (*right*) and PC George Cordery in 1964. PC Fielder joined the force in 1949, having previously been a Military Policeman. He was appointed as a dog handler in 1957 but did not attend his Elementary Dog Handlers course until 1963. PC Cordery joined in 1950. He had previously been in the RAF. He was appointed to the dog section in 1957 and his course was in 1959.

**112** Shanklin Police Station, Isle of Wight. This was built in 1951 and was the first purpose-built police station in the town. Previously all police business was conducted from the police house of the local police sergeant.

**113** Southampton County Borough Police, Civic Centre, *c.*1960. Picture taken in the parade room of Civic Centre Police Station. Appointments, handcuffs, truncheon and notebook were produced for Inspector Joe Skelton (*shown on the right*), Sergeants Les Watkins and, furthest from the camera, Sergeant Nelson Huggett. Sgt Huggett was a Lieutenant in the Provost Corps during the war. Constables on the left included Graham Troke, Dudley Bridgewater, Ken Martin, Brian Swain and Fred Dowrick. Each Civic Centre shift comprised an Inspector, two sergeants and 14 police constables.

**114** WPS 1 Doris Cole, Southampton Borough Force, outside Civic Centre Police Station. Doris Cole was the first Police Woman to be attested in 1942, and became the first Woman Police Sergeant. She retired in January 1965. There had previously been policewomen in 1915, when a Miss Tate was appointed. However, they were never attested and so had none of the police powers that Doris Cole would have had. On 17 December 1945 the Chief Constable commended Doris Cole. She was called to a public house where a prostitute had threatened to shoot another woman. Doris searched the young lady and recovered a loaded revolver from her pocket.

**115** PC 93 Arthur Bowe on motorcycle patrol on the A272 near Winchester in 1963. PC Bowe was appointed to Traffic Department in 1962 and later served at Basingstoke, Winchester, and Southampton. He retired in 1983.

**116** The newly opened Hampshire Police Headquarters in Winchester in 1966. It is still the headquarters of Hampshire Constabulary although accommodation is becoming even more cramped and departments are being moved to new locations.

**117** The opening of the new Hampshire and Isle of Wight Police Headquarters, West Hill, Winchester by HRH Princess Margaret, 1966. The senior officer nearest the camera is ACC John Wilkins. He joined the Bristol Police in 1939 before doing war service with the Dragoon Guards. In 1964 he was appointed Assistant Chief Constable of Southampton City Police.

**118** Havant Division cricket team, winners of the Major Warde Cup in 1968. The competition was inter-Division and named after the former Chief Constable Major Warde.
*Back row* (*left to right*): DCC J. Broomfield, Supt. L. Bowen, DCs Gale and Wright, PCs Chessell, Lacey, Peace, DS Wenden, C/INS Soper.
*Front row*: DC Dowling, PS Beacham, PC Green, PS Bulbeck, PS Mew, PC Peake.
Len Soper went on to become the Chief Constable of Gloucestershire.
Major A.B. Warde was Chief Constable of Hampshire from 1894 until 1928.

**119** The official opening in 1967 of Basingstoke Police Station. Phillip Allen is accompanied by the Divisional Commander, Chief Superintendent Wilf Burton. The original police station in New Street was also Police Headquarters of the Basingstoke Borough Police, formed in 1836 but abolished on 1 April 1889, when it amalgamated with Hampshire Constabulary.

**120** Display of Police Transport in the back yard of the new Basingstoke Police Station, London Road, at its opening in 1967.

**121** Woman Police Sergeant Joan Scott, around 1968, outside Portsmouth Central Police Station, Winston Churchill Avenue. The style of cap she is wearing was part of women's uniform at the time of the amalgamation of Portsmouth, Southampton and Hampshire forces in 1967.

**122** Hampshire Police control room at Police Headquarters. PC Eric Perriment, writing, was awarded the Queen Elizabeth II Silver Jubilee Medal in 1977 before his retirement in October that year. He then continued to work in the control room as a civilian telephonist. On the far right is PC Alec Ashbolt, who joined Southampton force in 1950, having previously been a Police Messenger, transferring on amalgamation in 1967. The control room at that time was situated on the third floor of Headquarters. The date is about 1968.

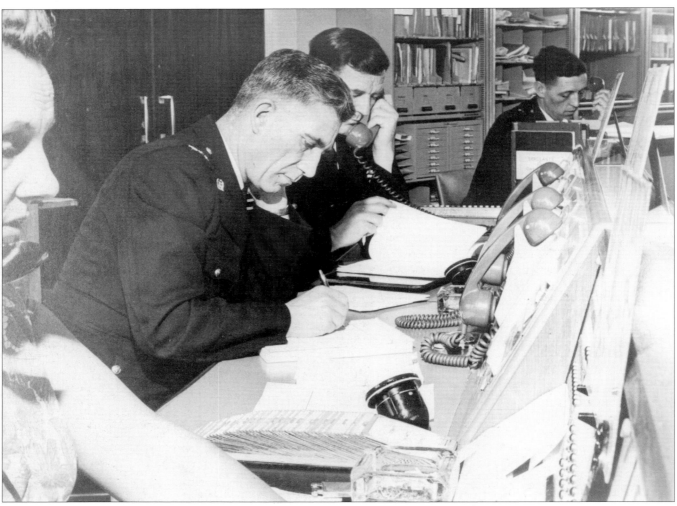

**123** WPC Sheila Sansom and colleague. Note the hefty typewriter to complete reports. Picture taken in about 1969.

**124** Southsea Police Station, Albert Road, Portsmouth was built in 1872. The building was vacated by the police in 1948 to facilitate rebuilding and modernisation. The refurbished station opened in 1956. In 1993 the police moved out never to return and the building became a public house, the *Fuzz and Firkin*, in 1996.

**125**　Traffic motorcyclists and a rural beat motorcyclist confer whilst policing the Isle of Wight Pop Festival on 26 August 1970.

**126**　Chief Constable Douglas Osmond at the Isle of Wight Pop Festival in 1970.
He started his career in the Metropolitan Police before the war. During the war he joined the Royal Navy and was later seconded to the Control Commission in Germany. He was appointed Chief Constable of Shropshire in 1946. He joined Hampshire Constabulary as Chief Constable in 1962 until his retirement in 1977. He still lives at Christchurch.

**127** Special events call for extra police resources. Reinforcements of Hampshire officers arrive on the Isle of Wight for the Isle of Wight Pop Festival in 1970. Chief Superintendent John Wheeler, the senior officer on the ground, is about to deploy officers. In the foreground are an unmarked police mini and a lightweight motorcycle, used by detached beat officers. John Wheeler is still the compère for concerts given by the Hampshire Constabulary Choir.

**128** Cadet training at Police Headquarters, Winchester. Seated nearest the camera is Mick Butcher. Mick is still serving as a Detective Constable on Special Branch.

**129** A posse of Mini Pandas leaving Bitterne Police Station, Whites Road, Southampton *c.*1968. Panda cars were introduced for Unit Beat Policing scheme. These mobile patrols supported foot and cycle beat officers. Panda cars got their name from the phrase 'Pursue and Arrest'. Bitterne Police Station was opened on 1 March 1965.

**130** Force Control Room in about 1971/2. On the left are Sergeant 140 Maurice Annetts, PC 774 Chris Richards, PC 503 Malcolm Gordon, PC 805 Bob Taylor and, farthest from the camera, PC 128 Colin Davey. On the right, second from the camera, is PC 2 Dennis Bennett.

**131**  Ford Cortina Patrol Car at Kingston Crescent Police Station in 1974.

**132**  Chief Constable Sir Douglas Osmond presenting WPC Julie Behrendt with a Probationer of the Year Trophy, 6 June 1973. When Julie was a sergeant she became the Force's first Visual Aids Officer preparing material for the trainers. Her training in Graphic Design at Portsmouth College of Art meant she was well qualified for the role. Julie went on to serve as Chief Inspector both at Southampton Central and Control Rooms before retiring in 2001.

**133**  The Priory at Bishop's Waltham became the Cadet Training School for the Hampshire Police in the early 1970s. Extensive training took place here and release to college was part of the curriculum. The training establishment provided a valuable programme between leaving full-time education and joining the police service as a constable. When the cadet programme was discontinued, the Priory became the Force Training School for all in-force training before the move in 1987 to the new training school at Netley. The old Priory has since been demolished. It was formerly inhabited by monks and during the Second World War was home to men of many nationalities serving Britain in the war effort.

**134**  PC Ray Dommett requests a breath test from a motorist. 'Just blow into this bag, sir, one long steady breath.' This photograph was taken in 1973 outside Kingston Crescent Police Station and is posed, the 'motorist' being another officer, acting the part for the camera.

**135** Police launch *Ashburton* in about 1973, pictured here with a Royal Navy Rescue Whirlwind helicopter in the Solent. Ashburton was launched in 1971 and was a Keith Nelson design. At 40 foot with a fibreglass hull, it was powered by a Cummins 8-cylinder 4-stroke diesel engine. It had a top speed of 20 knots and was equipped with radar and a 60-channel VHF radio. The crew of 12 were split into three watches.

**136** The aftermath of the IRA bombing of Aldershot Army Barracks on 22 February 1972. To this date this was the most serious terrorist attack the county has ever had to deal with.

**137** The original Alton Police Station in the early '70s. Officers are parking a Granada area car. The police station was built in 1845 and was only replaced by a purpose-built station in 1978.

**138** Control Room staff used this large Control Vehicle in the 1970s to attend major incidents.

**139** Hampshire Constabulary Traffic Range Rover in 1975. These vehicles carried enormous amounts of equipment and were supplied with an extendable floodlight for use at the scene of accidents.

**140** In 1976 Southampton Football Club beat Manchester United 1-0 to win the FA Cup Final. On the following Sunday large numbers of police were present to keep order whilst the team paraded their trophy through the streets of Southampton. This picture shows Chief Inspector Ken Carter, but known as Nick. Amongst the Saints players (*second from the right*) is Peter Rodrigues, still a regular visitor, now as a spectator.

**141** The Senior Officers' Mess in 1977. From left to right, Deputy Chief Constable Hedley Phillips, Sir Douglas and Lady Osmond. The Senior Officers' Mess still meets three times a year and is now open to Chief Inspectors and above and to support staff of equivalent rank. At the time of the picture it was for police officers only and then only above Superintendent rank. Hedley Phillips OBE, QPM retired from Hampshire Constabulary in 1983 after 37 years of police service. Following his service in the Royal Marines during the war he joined Berkshire Constabulary in 1946. He transferred to Hampshire in 1964, as an Assistant Chief Constable. He was appointed Deputy Chief Constable in 1967.

**142** WPC 2209 Mary-Ann Allen pictured in Winchester in about 1977. The white-topped cap for policewomen was replaced by the protective bowler-style in the late 1980s.

(Picture courtesy of Southern News Service)

**143** W.D.C. Brenda Boddington (joined 1960) and P.C. Ken Marsh (joined 1954) assist a witness in compiling a photo-fit in 1978. Ken Marsh is still playing Bowls for the Hampshire Police Bowls team and has represented the Force nationally in this sport.

**144** Pig herding on the M3 motorway. Doing his impression of a toreador with a yellow jacket is Sergeant Roy Bayntun, now the section Inspector at Lymington. Picture taken on 23 December 1985.

**145** National Front demonstration outside HMP Winchester in 1979. Hampshire brought in reinforcements from the Metropolitan Police to deal with its biggest such demonstration for many years. The protesters were there as a result of the imprisonment of National Front leader Relf.

**146** Cowes Police Station was first opened in 1900 and was the Headquarters of Cowes sub-division. There had been a station before this in Sun Hill, Cowes.

**147** PC 1256 Alex Francombe, the Cycle Beat Officer for Bedhampton, pictured leaving Havant Police Station in the early 1980s. After spells in Portsmouth and at Hayling Island, Alex has now returned to Havant as the Station Sergeant.

**148** Rover SD1 Traffic Patrol Car pictured at Havant in 1982. The driver, PC Martin Dickens, retired in the 1990s. The passenger, PC Terry Stevens, is still serving and is now the Chief Inspector at Gosport Division.

**149** Police Unit outside Fratton Park in the early 1980s.

**150** Officers policing an industrial dispute at Esso, Fawley in 1983 which lasted for six weeks. On the left, with silver braid on his cap, is Assistant Chief Constable Stobart.

**151** Post-coding cycles at Fareham Police Station in 1982. The picture shows Divisional Officer Alan Spencer of the Special Constabulary. Alan Spencer, a former butcher and latterly council official with Fareham Borough Council, spent 32 years as a Special Constable before finally retiring in 1988.

**152** For many years the Volvo was the preferred Area Car for Hampshire. This picture was taken in about 1982 on Southsea seafront.

**153** *Left to right*: PC Colin Bowden, PC Jim Mowat and Sergeant Dave Holt, all members of the Force Weapon training team. This photograph was taken in the range on the top floor of Police Headquarters, Winchester in 1982.

**154** Hampshire Police Choir, 1983. During the black days of the first air raids on Portsmouth Jimmy Cracknell, a Special Inspector with the Portsmouth City Police, became the founding member and first conductor of the Portsmouth City Police Choir. The choir gave its first public performance at Portsmouth Guildhall in November 1940. From then on the choir went from strength to strength making regular appearances on BBC's 'Friday Night is Music Night' and singing throughout the UK and abroad. Following the amalgamation in 1967, the choir became the Hampshire Police Choir and celebrated 50 years of music in 1990. The choir still skilfully performs today under its musical director, Terri Barnett LTCL, LRAM. Audiences enthusiastically receive it wherever it appears.

**155** Chief Constable John Duke, CBE, QPM. John Duke came to Hampshire from Essex Police in 1977 and served until his retirement in August 1988. John Duke, born in Newcastle upon Tyne, joined the City of London Police in 1947. He transferred to Essex Police as their ACC in 1969. In 1972 he was promoted to Deputy Chief Constable with Essex and on 1 September 1977 he became Chief of Hampshire. Within a year of his retirement he died after a short illness. Married to Glenys, he had four daughters.

**156**   Ex-Superintendent Peter Wall talking to Sgt Jim Lovelock, PC Elton Jonnson and PC John Warner in 1983 at the Butser Country Fair near Petersfield.

**157**   A BBC Radio Solent radio phone-in with the local police at Kingston Crescent Police Station, Portsmouth. *Pictured from left to right*: Chief Superintendent Day, WPC Hemmings, Sergeant Russell Parke, PC Gray, WPC Rosie Ord, Detective Sergeant Terry Flood and PC Ted Sibley.

**158** During the miners' strike in 1984, Hampshire was
the first force to fly its Mutual Aid contingent to
Nottingham. Hampshire officers are embarking at
Eastleigh airport in this photograph.

**159** Sergeant Tony Davis supervises the return of fans
to the terraces at the Dell in 1985, Archers Road end,
before the major refurbishment and move to an all-
seater stadium.

**160** In 1985 Air Support in Hampshire was focused on the Edgely Optica,
built at Old Sarum near Salisbury. Flying trials for the aircraft began in May
from H.M.S. *Daedalus* airstrip at Lee on the Solent. The aircraft, which was
leased from Airfoil, was officially handed over to the Air Support Unit on
14 May 1985. Within 24 hours the euphoria was replaced by a catastrophic
shock when the aircraft crashed at Ringwood, fatally injuring PC Gerry
Spencer and DC Malcolm Wiltshire, the two police officers who were
crewing the plane. They had been recording traffic flows for the Ringwood
Market at the time of the crash. The Optica G-BMPL is photographed here
over the Needles. In March 1990, following a power failure, the Optica was
grounded. In May, the same year, the Air Support Unit took possession of
the Pilatus Britten Norman Islander G-TWOB. This aircraft has been the
backbone of the unit since that date.

**161** Hampshire Constabulary launch *Ashburton*, photographed off Southsea. This vessel was replaced by three smaller ones in 1995.

**162** The Police Station in St Peters Road, Petersfield. The wall plaque on its frontage indicates its origins as 1858, although it is believed to have been built some years previously. Formerly a divisional headquarters, it is now an inspectors' station. The former courthouse at the rear is now a museum. On the social side many will remember the balls held yearly by the Petersfield police at the town hall featuring the big bands of the day, such as those of Joe Loss and Jack Parnell.

**163** BMW 528i Traffic Patrol Car pictured outside of Police Headquarters, Winchester, 1987.

**164** P.S. Mike Adkins (Whitchurch) and P.C. Nick Cave (Basingstoke) on borrowed horses performing duty at Aldershot Football Club in 1988 when they were still in the football league. The Hampshire mounted branch had terminated on the introduction of motor vehicles in the 1920s and Southampton followed suit in the 1930s.

**165** PC Kevin Joyner, Traffic motorcyclist at Portsmouth, riding a BMW R80.

**166** Fordingbridge Police Station (1988) was built in Station Road in 1857.
At one time, in keeping with other market towns, Fordingbridge had its own magistrates' court. This was closed in 1955 and cases are now heard at Ringwood. In days past the town was busy; the September fair was a favourite meeting and drinking occasion, for which police officers were drafted in.

**167** 150 years of Hampshire Constabulary was marked in 1989 by a service of thanksgiving at Winchester Cathedral. A new Force Standard was dedicated. This photo shows Sergeant Bob Rose superimposed above a floodlit Cathedral. Bob Rose is now a Chief Inspector at Headquarters.

**168** Retired officers taking part in the march-past at Winchester Cathedral celebrating 150 years of Hampshire Constabulary. Those pictured include Graham 'Nick' Carter, George Williams, Peter Kingston, 'Steve' Stevens, Graham Swain, John Lee, Ray 'Wiggy' Bennett, Ken Price, Derek Jackson and Dave Bartlett. The commander leading the contingent is Ron Godden, senior.

**169** March-past of the Hampshire Constabulary at Winchester Cathedral to celebrate the Force's 150th Anniversary. Leading the procession is ACC Bryan Davies, followed by Sergeant Bob Rose (carrying the standard) and Inspector Ron Godden, shouting a command to the column. Bryan Davies joined Southampton City Police in 1949 and transferred to Hampshire on amalgamation as an Inspector. He was appointed Assistant Chief Constable of Hampshire in 1983. In 1989 he was awarded the OBE before retiring in 1991.

**170** Jill Dando, Crimewatch UK presenter, with Detective Constable Norman Bundy and Detective Inspector Pete Shand. They were publicising Operation Pentagon, an investigation into a series of serious sexual assaults in Portsmouth between 1987 and 1988. As a result of the investigation and publicity a man was arrested and subsequently sentenced to 18 years' imprisonment on each of eight charges.

**171** Hampshire Traffic motorcyclist, Sergeant Phil Horn, on a BMW K100 at Emsworth in 1988. He retired in 2001 as the Chief Inspector on the Isle of Wight.

**172** Detective Chief Inspector Trevor Witt showing the Duchess of York the work of the Scientific Support Services within the Palmerston Building of Netley. Chief Constable John Hoddinott looks on. Taken in 1990 at the official opening.

**173** Hampshire Police Choir. Pictured left to right in the front row are: Clive Chamberlain, Geoff Culbertson, Brian Scarth, Trevor Barnes, Steve Hellier, Bill Bowskill. Left to right in the rear row are: John Mew, Tony Grenfell, Ken Malcolm, Bob Dowse and Mike Brooker. The conductor is Trevor Ibbotson.

**174** An attestation ceremony at Netley in 1991. Left to right: the Rev. Mike Stamford (Force Chaplain), Mr Stanley (Magistrate), Inspector Mick Gill (Probationer Training), Sergeant Dick Ironmonger (Probationer Training) with PC 1847 James Chapman being sworn in. Mike Stamford left the force in 1999. Inspector Gill retired from the force in 1998, but continued in the same job as a civilian until he finally retired in 2001. Sergeant Ironmonger is now an Inspector in the control room, whilst PC Chapman is now a Traffic Patrol officer at Fareham.

**175** The Air Support Unit in 1990 with the Islander plane at HMS *Daedalus*. *Left to right*: Pilot John Davies, PC Phil Wheeler, PC Barry Smith, PC Tony Abrams, Sgt Eric Hills, Chief Inspector Bob Ruprecht. Bob Ruprecht has since retired from the police, but continues as the Unit Executive Officer and pilot.

**176**  Ex-Southampton City officers at the Southampton City Reunion in 1992. They are standing next to the renovated Southampton Roll of Honour. The Roll was originally unveiled in 1949 by Lord Mayor Blanchard at Southampton Magistrates Court. After many years the Roll had somewhat deteriorated and, after careful restoration by 'Friends of the Salvation Army', it was again unveiled at its present location within the Force Training School at Netley. Left to right: Bryan Davies (Assistant Chief Constable of Hampshire), Alfie Cullen (ex-Chief Constable of Southampton City), Ron Wilton, Ray Cartwright and Dave Pallett. Ron, Ray and Dave were all ex-Southampton City officers joining in 1964, 1962 and 1959 respectively. Dave Pallett, who was a Hampshire Cadet before joining, went on to become the Safety Officer at Southampton Football Club. Both Ron Wilton and Ray Cartwright are ever-present members of the Hampshire Constabulary Bowls Team.

**177**  Police vehicle display at the Emergency Services 'It's a Knockout' at Southsea in 1992. Hands raised is Sergeant Nick Green and looking at camera above the BMW is PC Kim Fenton. The BMW in the foreground was the first unmarked Traffic Patrol car fitted with video recording equipment and concealed 'blue lights' and 'police' signs.

**178** Hampshire Constabulary Blue Lamp motorcycle display team. *Left to right*: PC Les Bellinger; PC Clive Whitworth; Sgt Jonathan Stainton-Ellis; PC Kim Fenton; Inspector Ken Ellcome; Sgt Nick Green; PC Joe Morris; PC John Hiney; PC Tony Johnson.

**179** In 1992 two young men were seen on the roof of shops in the Upper High Street, Andover. Attempts were made to talk them down, but not before they had caused thousands of pounds worth of damage to property and police vehicles.

**180** This high visibility police van was used regularly in the early '90s to deter kerb crawlers in the Southampton Red Light district.

**181** PC 1623 Raymond Bloye, 31 years, meets Margaret Thatcher at the unveiling of the bronze statue of a Marine at Eastney. In the centre is Inspector Brian Readwin, a member of Mrs Thatcher's security team. PC Bloye, who was born in Rayleigh in Essex, served as a Royal Marine between 1978 and 1987. He received the Falklands War Medal for his part in that conflict. At the time of the photograph (July 1992) he was serving at Southampton Central, although in 1993 he transferred to Kent County Constabulary.

**182** PC Mick Lyons was the first officer to be permanently posted to a school in Hampshire. He worked at Oaklands Comprehensive School in Havant. The picture shows him launching his third major appeal for charity. After his mother died of cancer, Mick raised £1.4 million for a CT Scanner for the Queen Alexandra Hospital. His second appeal was for a Lithotripter (destroys kidney- and gallstones). This appeal, launched in 1993, was to raise enough cash to buy three special transport incubators for use in the neonatal and maternity units at St Mary's Hospital, Portsmouth. Mick was awarded the BEM for his charitable work. He still raises money for charity at the QA Hospital.

**183** Eugenie Hampton, pictured on her retirement from Hampshire Federation of Victim Support Schemes in 1994, with John Hoddinott, Chief Constable. On her death in 1997, the Hampton Trust was set up in her memory.

**184** Hampshire Constabulary Band, taken at one of their many concerts. *Back row* (*left to right*): Dawn Morgan (bassoon); Liz Gosney and Bob Scarrett (horns). *Front row* (*left to right*): Emma Dodge and David Basson (oboes); Liz Brunt and Amanda Jane Osman (clarinets).

**185** The Princess Royal accompanied by members of the Hampshire Constabulary including Sergeant Craig McIntosh; in civilian clothes following behind the Princess is DC Mick Butcher. The picture was taken at Cowes on the Isle of Wight.

**186** Hampshire Constabulary's Southern Support and Training Headquarters, Netley. Previously part of the Royal Victoria Military Hospital, it now houses the Training School and conference facilities.

**187** Police Land Rover being driven by PC Guy Ripon.

**188** ACC Bryan Davies gives a speech at the leaving party of Deputy Chief Constable Michael Mylod on 23 April 1995. Michael Mylod joined the Northern Rhodesia Police in 1957 and rose to the rank of Inspector. When he returned to this country he joined Devon and Cornwall Police and served with them until in 1984 he was appointed Assistant Chief Constable of Avon and Somerset. In 1988 he became the Deputy Chief Constable of Hampshire. When he retired Mr Mylod took up post as the Commissioner of Police for Bermuda before returning to retirement in Hampshire where he is still a member of the Senior Officers' Mess. Chief Constable John Hoddinott looks on.

**189** These firearms have been surrendered to the police and were guarded by members of the Tactical Firearms Team until they were sent for destruction. The crouching figure is Mark Benham, then a member of staff in the Firearms Licensing Department, but now a constable at Shirley. The escorting officers are Sergeant Martin 'Butch' Wilkins (*left*) and PC Tony Hatcher (*right*). The officers are armed with the Heckler and Koch MP5 carbine and in their holsters are Smith and Wesson self-loading pistols. This is the normal weaponry carried by the TFT, whilst the Armed Response Units only carry the MP5.

**190** Sergeant Ricky Burrows demonstrates the use of the ASP to a group of officers. WPC Antonia Weeks, WPC Kerry Henderson, PC Paul Harfield, WPC Alison Dibdin, WPC Alison Macey, PC Colin Weeks and an unidentified PC. The ASP replaced the traditional wooden police truncheon in 1996.

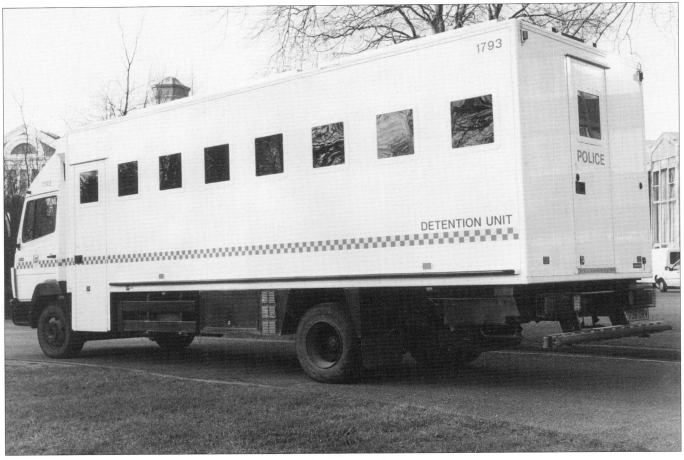

**191**   Hampshire Constabulary mobile detention unit. This almost became redundant in 1997 when movements between police stations and prisons were passed to the private sector. The vehicle was used for major public order incidents, but has since been converted into an exhibition vehicle.

**192**   Rover 820 Area Car used until the mid-1990s.

**193**  Taken in 1996 at Whitehill, this picture shows PC Guy Milton (*left*) with his son-in-law WO1 Dale Pitt (RMP). PC Chris White is showing the patrol car to Sergeant Keith Trigwell of the Australian Military Police. Sgt Trigwell was on secondment to the RMP.

**194**  Sergeant Clifford Williams shows the Home Secretary Michael Howard around Basingstoke on 15 July 1996. Clifford, a member of the Hampshire Constabulary History Society, is now an Inspector working at Bramshill.

**195**  The new Force Control Vehicle. The officer on the right is Sergeant Dave Bourne who has since transferred to Kent Police. Based at the Force Control Room, this vehicle is deployed to major events such as Pop Festivals, major incidents and force exercises. Fully equipped with radio and telephone links, it has working area for the police commander as well as a room for the control room staff who operate the communications equipment.

**196** Prince Edward meeting WPC Naomi Crees-Smith at Netley. WPC Crees-Smith was given the various campuses of the Southampton University as her beat in the mid-1990s.

**197** Hampshire Constabulary Band photographed at the rear of Netley Training School. The Band comprises both serving and retired police and support staff members of the force and has played nationally and internationally. Based at Netley, it has a very full programme of events every year, which are always well attended. The Director of Music is Len Lewry, a serving officer stationed at Cosham.

**198** The launch of the Zero Tolerance Domestic Violence campaign in Southampton in 1997. *Left to right are*: Superintendent Chris Lee (now ACC Dorset), Chief Superintendent Roger Honey (now Southampton City Council Community Safety Manager), Chief Inspector Derek Stevens, Steph Atkinson (Southampton City Council), Inspector Zen Stopinski, Inspector John Kenna and Superintendent Graham Wyeth. Derek Stevens is the current Chairman of the Hampshire Constabulary History Society.

**199** John Bradley, Transport Manager, Cyril Fellowes (Workshop Manager) and Ron Culver (Police Authority) look on as Gavin Bartlett celebrates the Government decision, in 1997, not to enforce Competitive Compulsory Tendering to Police Vehicle Fleet Maintenance. The Force and Transport Manager, John Bradley, has won many accolades for Vehicle and Fleet Management in the national arena.

**200** A lot of the jobs previously done by police officers are now undertaken by support staff including preparing files for court. Pictured here are Mark Thomas and Vanessa Coleville at Bitterne Police Station in the Admin Support Unit.

**201** PC Simon Wright made national news by booking over 7,000 motorists in a year at Basingstoke with the new radar camera speed gun.

**202** Sergeant Howard Norman with his Alsatian, Sammy, both wearing their ballistic vests in 1996. The ballistic vest for the dog was on trial from the manufacturers, but has since been returned as it proved to be too heavy and bulky for the dog and could not be worn for more than about five minutes.

**203** Special Constable 321 Amanda Paice from Havant dealing with a cyclist. The Force continues to encourage the recruitment of Special Constables. They are equipped to similar levels as their regular colleagues and receive comprehensive training, mainly undertaken at weekends and in the evenings.

**204** *Earl Mountbatten of Burma*, one of three new craft for the Hampshire Marine Unit. These three smaller craft replaced the Police launch *Ashburton*, and are based at Cowes, Southampton and Gosport.

**205** The new Meon Valley Police Station. Opened in 1996, it is staffed by an Inspector, two sergeants, 20 constables, a support staff Station Enquiry Officer, and a cleaner. It is built on the same site as the old police station, which was a converted dwelling house, in Hoe Road, Bishop's Waltham.

**206** Sergeant Stash Falinski with his mountain bike. He is better known for his work as the Football Liaison Officer at Fratton Park, home of Portsmouth Football Club.

**207** Volvo T5, winter scene 1997. The Volvo T5 is the preferred vehicle for Traffic Patrol in Hampshire. Several are also equipped with 'gun boxes' as they double up as Armed Response Vehicles. The Volvo has an excellent safety record and is capable of a top speed of 145 miles per hour. They are basically production models, with only the brakes uprated because of the high speeds at which the vehicle has to travel.

**208** John Hoddinott and his wife Avril with daughters Rebecca (*left*) and Louise (*right*) at Buckingham Palace when he received his knighthood in 1998.

**209** The Policy Group, photographed at Netley. *Left to right*: Detective Chief Superintendent Keith Akerman, Chief Superintendents Gerry French, Colin Smith, Phil Scott, Roger Honey and David Basson in the back row. In the front row, ACCs Ian Readhead, Peter Jones, Chief Constable John Hoddinott, and Deputy Chief Constable Bill Nelson. Peter Jones arrived in Hampshire as an ACC in 1991, having joined Cheshire Constabulary in 1968. He retired in 2000. Bill Nelson spent his career with the Metropolitan Police, joining in 1968. He transferred to Hampshire as an ACC in 1991 and also retired in 2000.

**210** Detective Superintendent David Hanna (with briefcase) is followed down the stairs by murder suspect Victor Farrant arriving at Southampton Airport after successful extradition proceedings. Farrant was later convicted of murder and attempted murder in 1998.

**211** In 1999 the BBC screened a documentary following the public and private lives of Gosport police officers. Shown here are some of the stars: WPC Kris Allen, Inspector Clive Ayling, PC Ross Freemantle, DS Nigel Oliver and Superintendent Peter Baldry.

**212** In 1999 Hampshire Police were required to 'protect' Mary Chipperfield as she left Aldershot Magistrates Court where she had been found guilty of cruelty to animals.

**213** The police mobile column at the Farnborough Air Show. This air show attracts huge crowds and flying and ground exhibits from all around the world. In order to deal with traffic, crowds and potential emergencies there is always a large police presence in and around the show.

**214**  The Islander Police Aircraft G-HPAA. Hampshire is one of the few police forces in the country to opt for a fixed wing aircraft in preference to a helicopter. This Islander, owned by Hampshire Police between 1992 and 2001, was powered by Lycoming piston engines and was capable of 120 knots. In 2001 it was sold to a firm in Louisiana, USA, who will use it for spraying mosquitoes. The new Defender 4000 version of the Britten Norman Islander currently in service is powered by Rolls Royce Allison turbine engines and is capable of 140 knots.

**215**  Chief Constable Sir John Hoddinott CBE, with Home Secretary Michael Howard. Although born and bred in Hampshire, he chose to join the Metropolitan Police in 1961, rather than follow the footsteps of his father, Leslie, and grandfather, Samuel, who were both members of Hampshire Constabulary. He was appointed Assistant Chief Constable in Surrey in 1981, before joining Hampshire as DCC in 1983. He was appointed Chief Constable in September 1988 when John Duke retired. In 1998 he became Sir John when he was awarded his knighthood. He retired in 1999.

**216**  The purpose-built Control Room, Vickery House, named after a Crimean soldier. This building now houses all the four control rooms for the two counties. It is built in the grounds of Netley and is in the same style as Victoria House, the training school. All 999 calls for both counties are now received in this building. It was officially opened by HRH The Princess Royal on 22 October 2001.

**217** In the centre is Sergeant Kelvin Shipp, Secretary of the HCHS, outside Portsmouth Central Police Station, during the filming of an 'Eastenders' episode. Also pictured are WPC Alison Hart and PC Darren Doyle. The picture shows the variety of uniform currently in use. You can see that the two constables have rigid handcuffs, an extendable baton (ASP) and a holster for their CS Spray. The high visibility anorak being worn by the female officer is both waterproof and reflective and used mainly by Traffic officers. The traditional 'combed' helmet is still the preferred headgear for foot patrol, whilst the peaked cap is for mobile patrol. Finally the 'bowler' style reinforced hat is specified for female officers. Both constables wear a 'utility belt' to 'store' their appointments, including radio and first-aid pouches.

**218** Chief Constable Paul Kernaghan joined the force from North Yorkshire in 2000.

# INDEX

Figures in **bold** refer to illustration page numbers.